Zoë Foster (Blake) likes to thi. because she is always scripting messages to guys for friends, has a fantastic mum who is a Real Life psychologist, comes with plenty of personal experience and has been employed as *Cosmopolitan's* dating columnist since 2009. She has worked in women's magazines for over a decade, and loves nothing more than lovingly bullying young dames into a genuine and heightened sense of self-confidence. She's the author of four novels, *Air Kisses*, *Playing the Field*, *The Younger Man* and *The Wrong Girl*, the best-selling beauty bible *Amazing Face*, and she reckons that top looks great on you.

Hamish Blake once got one side of a Rubik's Cube all the same colour and describes his knowledge of relationships as 'a touch less successful than that'. Which is okay, because all he has to do in this book is reveal what guys think, and he has been a guy since he was born, and technically even a little bit before then. He co-hosts the national radio show *Hamish and Andy*, presents the travel TV show *Hamish and Andy's Gap Year* and is the author of *Dave and Hamish Hate Girls* (written at age 7), although his hardline stance on females has softened since the publication of that work.

TEXTBOOK ROMANCE

ZOË FOSTER
WITH HAMISH BLAKE

PENGUIN BOOKS

PENGUIN BOOKS

Published by the Penguin Group
Penguin Group (Australia)
707 Collins Street, Melbourne, Victoria 3008, Australia
(a division of Penguin Australia Pty Ltd)
Penguin Group (USA) Inc.
375 Hudson Street, New York, New York 10014, USA
Penguin Group (Canada)
90 Eglinton Avenue East, Suite 700, Toronto, Canada ON M4P 2Y3
(a division of Penguin Canada Books Inc.)
Penguin Books Ltd
80 Strand, London WC2R 0RL England
Penguin Ireland
25 St Stephen's Green, Dublin 2, Ireland
(a division of Penguin Books Ltd)
Penguin Books India Pvt Ltd
11 Community Centre, Panchsheel Park, New Delhi – 110 017, India
Penguin Group (NZ)
67 Apollo Drive, Rosedale, Auckland 0632, New Zealand
(a division of Penguin New Zealand Pty Ltd)
Penguin Books (South Africa) (Pty) Ltd, Rosebank Office Park, Block D,
181 Jan Smuts Avenue, Parktown North, Johannesburg, 2196, South Africa
Penguin (Beijing) Ltd
7F, Tower B, Jiaming Center, 27 East Third Ring Road North,
Chaoyang District, Beijing 100020, China

Penguin Books Ltd, Registered Offices: 80 Strand, London, WC2R 0RL, England

First published by Penguin Group (Australia), 2009
This edition published 2014

13 5 7 9 10 8 6 4 2

Text copyright © Zoë Foster Blake & Hamish Blake 2009

The moral right of the author has been asserted

All rights reserved. Without limiting the rights under copyright reserved above, no part of this
publication may be reproduced, stored in or introduced into a retrieval system, or transmitted, in any
form or by any means (electronic, mechanical, photocopying, recording or otherwise), without the prior
written permission of both the copyright owner and the above publisher of this book.

Typeset in Sabon by Post Pre-Press Group, Brisbane, Queensland
Printed and bound in Australia by McPherson's Printing Group, Maryborough, Victoria

National Library of Australia
Cataloguing-in-Publication data:

Textbook romance : a step-by-step guide to getting the guy
/ Zoë Foster Blake, Hamish Blake.
9780734311245
Dating (Social customs)--Handbooks, manuals, etc.
Man-woman relationships--Handbooks, manuals, etc.
Blake, Hamish.

646.77

penguin.com.au

CONTENTS

Module One: Preparation

Module Two: Dating

Module Three: Relationships

module one:
preparation

1.

Defining the Probability of Needing This Book

In this lesson, you'll learn whether you're a good candidate for relationship advice, or whether you could have just bought several packets of Fantales and not worried about this book.

Did you know Goldie Hawn was born on 21-11-45? Now we're just as good as Fantales.

You have purchased, stolen or been given this book because:

- You believe (or someone who knows you does) that you could benefit from some relationship advice.
- You are at a crossroads in your relationship.
- You buy guides and textbooks for every other aspect of your life – why not love?
- You're dyslexic and thought the title read *Teri Hatcher: A Biography.*

This book isn't for everyone. For instance, Grandpa, you should probably put it down. There are swear words and notions of sex.

It is for women (single, dating or in a Proper Relationship) who feel baffled and frustrated by men, or

I guarantee you, that didn't make Grandpa put it down – he just flicked ahead.

who know that, deep down, they could be happier in their romantic relationships.

It is for women who are DOING THEIR HEAD IN waiting for That Guy to call, or text, or email, or exhibit some sign of a pulse.

It is for women who 'always seem to end up with arseholes'.

It is for women who are bored of complaining to their girlfriends that they can't find a man. Or a decent one who doesn't play games.

It is for women who are sick of analysing their boyfriend's actions to the point of madness.

And it is for women who feel like they have lost themselves in their relationship.

It is for women who don't mind having a book that is pre-scribbled on, and doesn't appear to have been discounted for it.

In a series of simple lessons (and by simple I mean extraordinarily difficult) this book instructs you on how to be more in control of, more at peace with, and more successful in your romantic relationships. We used the textbook format for several reasons. One is so that you can refer back to pertinent lessons with ease when you need them. Another is because we wanted to make it absolutely transparent how important it is to possess an artillery of reliable strategy and intelligence if you want to find that elusive Perfect Relationship, and by being forced to learn it in a recognisably educational format, you're more likely to take it seriously and remember it. Finally, it's fun to make pie charts.

Also, it was easier than tracking down Ms Winston from your old high school to explain it to you. I wonder how old 'wobbles' Winston is doing these days . . . ?

You'll learn what it is you are doing to inhibit your happiness and your chances of a fulfilling relationship. You will learn how to deal with the fact that when it comes to biological wiring, men and women are roughly the same as a bedside lamp and a killer whale.

It won't all be sweets and slippery dips, though – the rebuilding of your confidence and fostering of an understanding of how this all works requires dedication and the valuing of long-term satisfaction over instant gratification.

Then you can have some sweets and slippery dips.

TAKE A TEST

For the following questions, award yourself 22.1 points for every 'Yes' and 14.6 for every 'No'.

Are you:
Unhappily single?
Happily single?
Releasing a single?
Unhappily single but pretending you're happily single?
Single because every time you're offered a shot at love you freak out?
Single because he is incapable of committing to more than just casual sex?
Dating a guy who is doing your head in?
Dating a guy whose head *you* are doing in?
In a new relationship?
In a new relationship you're worried you may ruin?
In a new relationship that he is sabotaging day by day?
In a new relationship but angry he won't admit to it on Facebook?
In a relationship that has lost its excitement?
In a solid relationship that doesn't seem to be progressing?
In a solid relationship that features the same fights again and again?
In a solid relationship with a wobbly looking future?

In a solid relationship that needs some refreshing?
In a solid relationship but considering breaking out?
In a solid-steel shipping crate?

If your final answer was a number over 14.6, then this book is definitely something you should read, underline furiously and read again.

Or buy a new copy to underline again and again. I promise this suggestion to re-purchase the book has nothing to do with the fact that I would like a new television.

Also, at the end of each chapter, if there's some room left and no one is looking, I may actually have some sort of thought on the topic discussed in the chapter. I can't guarantee I'll have one every time, but if I do, I'll pounce on it. Nor can I guarantee these thoughts will be of the highest quality, as we can see by this one, which is essentially just a promise to try and have more thoughts. Enjoy the book.

2.

Be Honest About Yourself

In this lesson, you'll learn that the most crucial part of being happy in a relationship is first ensuring you're in terrific form yourself.

THE BASICS

- You already know all of this stuff.
- You probably don't do any of it.
- Don't bother reading the rest of the book if you're not going to pay attention to this chapter.

One thing that constantly lets women down before they even commence dating, or even begin looking for a man (*wrong*, see Module One, Lesson 6), is that they haven't got their own shit together first. This can also be true for women who find themselves in an unhappy relationship. It means they haven't done enough work on themselves, and are not yet in the confident, self-loving state of mind that forms the basis of every Quality Relationship.

Clues that you don't have your shit together include:

you'd be amazed at how quickly guys can detect a girl who isn't mentally balanced, which is highly hypocritical of us seeing as we're the gender that commits the most crimes, starts all the wars, etc ...

- You don't feel you deserve a good man, because you'll only ruin things anyway.
- On Facebook, you're still 'In a Relationship' with your ex, even though you've been single for six weeks.
- You coast past 'your' man's house to see if he's making out with some tart on the sofa. Eighteen months after you broke up with him.
- You have spent all of your precious 'single' time obsessing over undesirable men in your past, unattainable men in the present, or possible men in your future, rather than taking time to understand why you seem to have the same issues in every relationship (insecurity, jealousy, nonchalance, flatulence) and working out how you can rectify them.
- You haven't been single since you were 14 because you leapfrog from one relationship to the next.
- You get smashed, have a one-night stand and then cry all the next day.
- You get smashed, have a one-night stand and then do it again the next night.
- You broke up with your ex three days ago and bought this book because it was either that or a tattoo.
- You're in a relationship but you're envious of your single friends.
- You found a new man before you ended it with the last one and, *holy shit*, he's not as amazing as he seemed when you were cheating on your ex with him.
- You've been married four times.

By the way: just hiding these things doesn't count. They're coming off you like those invisible stink lines you see in comics.

While there isn't space to go into great detail here about *how* to get your shit together, we can have a run through the basics.

So while you're sitting there waiting for your fake tan to dry (I know I am) and wondering why you're not in a Quality Relationship, there are a few things you might consider to ensure that you're ready for romancification (and as a bonus, they'll also improve your life, your popularity, your career prospects and your chances of becoming a finalist on a televised singing competition).

ARE YOU HAPPY WITH YOURSELF?

Do you make the most of your looks? Your face, teeth, hair? Are you clean? Do you use deodorant? Do you smile much? Are you polite? Do you have good manners? Are you motivated in life? Healthy? Fit? Are you interesting? Do you have hobbies (watching *E! News* doesn't count)? Do you live in a dignified place? Are you kind? Do you take time to learn new things? Are you open to new people, places and experiences? (Tennis, seeing live music, daylight?) Finally, most importantly: *Are you the very best person you can be?*

If you answered no to one or more of these, then you need to get to work making some changes. Not least because probably the biggest and happiest consequence of feeling happy within yourself is that it makes you attractive.

I have a friend who we'll call Pearl. (To protect the innocent – and even the guilty – I'll use names from early last century.) Pearl liked to sit and tell me how miserable she was because she'd put on weight and she

If you answered 'yes' to everything, my housemate wants to date you. If you answered 'beans' he still wants to date you, but it gives you an idea of his standards ...

felt gross and unsexy, and the idea of getting naked for a man sent shivers down her spine. We had this conversation at least once a week. And then one day I slapped her across the face with an oven mitt and told her TO SNAP OUT OF IT AND LOSE THE GOD-DAMN WEIGHT ALREADY. I didn't really do that, of course, but I did tell her she was boring and I no longer wanted to be invited to her pity party. And that her weight gain (actually quite minimal) was banned from conversation.

Guys run a mile from girls like Pearl – not because of the oven-mitt mark on her face (I don't believe Zoë didn't hit her – I've seen her angry), but because she's practically telling them to.

Here's a list of things you need to do to ensure you're happy with yourself and that will massively maximise your attractiveness to others:

1. Love yourself

It is *impossible* to love anyone else until you love yourself. If you're aware that you're unhappy within yourself for any reason, work on it. Fix it. Get that self-esteem soaring. Living a life fighting with yourself or your flaws is a life half-lived.

2. Look good, feel amazing

For some people, physical confidence comes from eating well or yoga. For others, it's a new haircut. For others still, it means a nose job, hair extensions, a signature scent, tops that hide their tuckshop arms, or a noisy pink lipstick. *Whatever makes you look excellent, will make you feel excellent.* There's *nothing* that can take away the elevated mood and self-esteem that accompanies looking your Best Possible You. So get onto it.

3. Check your emotional IQ

If you oscillate wildly between being deadly calm and psychotic, or flip your lid at the smallest sign of stress, or wear tight glittery T-shirts that say 'TTL Bitch 'n Proud of It!', there's a good chance you will not be adequately equipped to handle the emotional rollercoaster that is dating and relationships. This is heavy stuff! Potentially gut-wrenching, mind-blowing, heartbreaking stuff. Emotional stability and intelligence, and the ability to be calm and confident in tense or pressured situations, are fantastically attractive qualities.

4. Enjoy your life

It sounds so clichéd. But have a good, hard look at your life right now: is it fun? Is your spare time spent bored or listless or frustrated, or is it spent doing things and spending time with people who are engaging, interesting and motivating? It's impossible to develop a healthy, happy relationship unless you have a full, rich and rewarding life as a single woman. Girls who glow get the guys.* Ladies with a zest for life are irresistible.

*Like a lighthouse, except we want to crash into you. (Clumsy analogy. Should have gone for candle and moth.)

5. Sass the confidence

When you believe in yourself, others believe in you. When you feel like you have something to offer, others can't help but be intrigued and attracted. Put it like this: be the girl in the room enjoying yourself the most. People want to earn the interest of the girl who values herself with such high regard.

6. Love men

If you hope to attract one, you kind of have to think of them as nice. And why wouldn't you? Men are

Like in Mr Men books (let me know if I'm getting too intellectual): if you hate Mr Grumpy (who doesn't?), why not go out with Mr Tickle? I mean, imagine what he could do with those hands ...

wonderful creatures. One even half-*made* you! Man-haters reveal so much more about themselves than men, with their venom-soaked rants about how all men are liars/cheats/bacteria. Be wary of signs you're becoming one of them. And if a man hurt you in the past, relegate the crime to That Man, not all men.

Important: *Don't be fooled into thinking this is a List of Perfection that you must fulfil before a man could possibly be interested in you.* It's not about being a size 8 with perfect rows of gleaming white pegs, who is Tina Fey at dinner parties and a marathon runner on the weekends. It's about knowing when you feel your best, when you feel your happiest and most attractive, and making that your regular state.

If you don't spend some time working on yourself and getting yourself to a level of self-love that would dazzle even the undazzleable, you'll risk trying to fill your Blank Spaces with a man, and tumble into bad relationships.

DATING DICTIONARY: BLANK SPACES

Or as I like to call them, '— —'.

Blank Spaces are areas in your life where something is missing – something seemingly man-shaped. Usually, but not always, they're emotional voids. Typical Blank Spaces include: wanting a more exciting or glamorous life, wanting to be happier, wanting to be more confident, wanting more self-worth, and wanting access to sex on a regular basis. If your life has Blank Spaces, **only you can fill them.** Expecting a man to fill these areas *will not work.* Shut up. It won't.

TYPICAL FEMALE BLANK SPACES

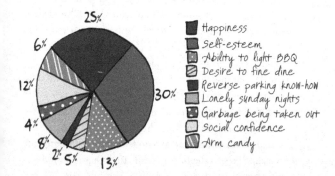

Consider Shy Ruth. She always *wanted* to be a super-spontaneous, fun, outgoing person, and do wild things like swim out beyond where her feet could touch the sand, attend large outdoor concerts and eat asparagus. When she met Bold Bernie he was all of this and more. He was gregarious, funny, loud and always up for something new. He even had *facial hair*! Ruth thought that they were a match made in heaven because he was all the things she was not – he made her feel confident and alive, and Paula Abdul had once taught her that in love, opposites attract. But pretty soon Bernie got tired of always having to be the fun one, the one who thought up new ideas, the one who booked for the scuba diving lessons. He grew resentful that Ruth didn't bring anything to the relationship that excited and invigorated *him*. She was always, 'Whatever *you* want to do . . . I'll have whatever *you're* having'. And despite Bernie's best efforts to bring out her hunger for life, Ruth remained reliant on him. Eventually it became so tiresome that Bernie broke up with her and soon after hooked up with Crazy Cynthia, a nude bungee jumper from Queenstown who shared his dream of setting up a beanie shop at the base of Mt Everest.

It's normal to be attracted to a man because he offers what you feel you lack – because you sense he (or the relationship) will 'help' you get back your self-esteem, or confidence.

But when you depend on a man to fill the Blank Spaces you have in your life, it usually ends in an imbalance, because one person feels they're bringing all the cupcakes to the person while the other is a mad pig who just keeps jamming them in their mouth and not even bothering to wipe the sprinkles from their lips.

Add that to the fact that we find it incredibly hard to make cupcakes in the first place, and you see the problem.

However! If Ruth had worked on her outgoingness by attending rock climbing classes or joining an asparagus-eating club *before* she had met Bernie, and then continued to actively thrust herself into being as equally adventurous as he was, the relationship would have had a much stronger chance of survival. As it turned out, she was depending on Bernie too much, and as anyone who has ever had to hold a newborn baby knows – having to support their bendy little necks and floppy legs while they sit there doing nothing and being all pathetic – there is such a thing as being *too* dependent.

In other words, guys don't want to go out with someone who is too easily impressed by them. We don't just want a fan, we want a play pal, too.

Sit down, examine honestly what you feel your Blank Spaces are, and genuinely do your best to fill them, or at least be aware what they are so you can start working on them. Write a list. Write one *write now*. (Puns are great, aren't they? I don't know who would ever say they were sarcasm's cheap, whorey sister.)

Seriously, though. Go on, write your list. And be brutally honest: if subconsciously – or consciously – you go for men with nice cars and an exciting social life that you want a piece of, write that down. The small effort it takes to do this will pay literally *millions* of make-believe dollars in dividends when you decide you are ready for a Quality Relationship.

> ### Mini Lesson: Perspective is Key, or Being Single is Fucking Awesome
>
> Like everything in life – especially losing vast amounts of money at foreign casinos – being single is all about perspective. It is a small window of time (it'll be *really* small once you've read this book) to re-evaluate and renovate yourself.
>
> It is time to blossom emotionally, socially and mentally. Time to read self-help books with exclamation marks in the title (like *I'm OK! You're OK! Both of Us Could Probably Be Doing Better!*) and to understand who YOU are, without spending 50–98% of your energy wondering or worrying about another human being.
>
> Time to wear fake tan to bed without getting into trouble for your potatoey stench and sticky, sheet-staining skin. And, of course, a time to be inappropriate on the dance floor with any man you choose and to get home and get up at whatever time you like.
>
> Never in your life can you be so utterly, deliciously selfish as when you are single. DO NOT PASS THIS OPPORTUNITY UP.
>
> But mostly it's about broadening your interests

This way you'll meet someone who is like you, not like the you who you think people might like. (So far the most confusing sentence of the book, but read it again, it makes sense.)

and expanding your mind. So don't waste it being sad or regretful or angry about relationships past. That's useless, destructive energy and time-wasting at its finest. Consider this: you're carrying around all those toxic thoughts and feelings about him, unable to sleep or eat or function properly, and he's waltzing around happy as a pig in shit, sparing no thought for you. Ouchy, but true – for as long as you let it be true.

WHAT HAVE YOU LEARNED?

Before you can attract a good man and a Quality Relationship, what *you* are putting on offer has to be awesome too. Realising this and doing something about it is not only helpful during the courting phase, and for happiness and longevity in your relationship, but for you as a human being. (Or for you as a robot. No judging here.)

Bonus analogy point, because guys really do like shiny, sharp tools. I mean that in the nicest way.

And note that if you don't bother to shine and sharpen your best tool (yourself, not your vegetable peeler), the rest of this book will be frustrating and largely useless, in the same way that using a spoon to comb your hair is, only with less spoon and hair, and more book.

So be terrifyingly honest about your flaws and your strengths, know your worth, build up your confidence, work on how you present yourself to the world and *love yourself to the point of wanting to text yourself sexy messages before bed.*

Guys don't have a clear idea in their head of the perfect girl they want, which you magically have to match. Firstly, the amount of brain power that would take is too much of a load on a mind already devoted to tracking several sporting seasons at once. Secondly, we love surprises (except after 60, then for coronary reasons we need warnings); we'll always be fascinated by what we haven't seen before. Would we rather go to the local school fete we've been to a dozen times before or a newly opened theme park called 'Awesomeland'? (I don't know what they've got in Awesomeland, but it sounds awesome.)

3.

The Perceived Value Theory

In this lesson, you'll learn that thinking of yourself as incredibly valuable means others will see you that way too. (You'll also learn that you're actually a designer bag made in France.)

The Mona Lisa is a prime example. Most expensive piece of art in the world because there's only one of them, even though the Dogs Playing Poker painting is funnier.

Perceived Value describes how things are only as valuable as people perceive them to be. The more rare things are, the more difficult they are to obtain, the more people think they are worth having.

I will explain this by way of leather goods, because I'm a girl. And all girls like leather goods. (And pillow fights and painting each others' nails.)

So. On your way to buy lunch, you see a handbag you like. It's the new season Chanel bag and it sizzles with splendour and sex. You're pretty sure your life will be at least 74% more wonderful if that bag is in it. People may ask you for autographs when you're seen with it. If you could buy it there and then and take it home and prop it up between your new season Fendi, Dior and YSL bags, chances are you would *enjoy* it but it wouldn't be something you *savoured*, something you considered special. It'd be Just Another Hot Bag.

On the other hand, if you had to save up for the bag, squirrelling away $100 a week for months, giving up your pokies and your stamp collecting and your love of throwing money into wishing wells, until it was almost *last season's* bag, when you finally got it home, it's likely you would cherish that bag more than the rest of your clothes, shoes and pets combined. Why? Because you had to work for it – it didn't come easily.

When things are challenging to obtain they appear more valuable, even if they are not actually 'better'. Even if that bag is made of the same leather as one that costs $80, and it's made by the same dingin' people, the price and the label give it an aura of desirability and unavailability. Luxury brands are so sought-after because they are only accessible to the 0.05% of the population.

The point is, you have to believe *you* are a Chanel bag. *You* are desirable. *You* stand out. Few people can afford you. You are hard to get.

Making yourself appear valuable is crucial, because not only do *you* start to believe it's true, *others* do too. A high Perceived Value is about confidence. It's the reason that some people who maybe don't set things alight aesthetically, or 'on paper', can enter a room and have everyone wanting to be their friend, or to be naked with them in bed, nibbling on their ears. A high Perceived Value is one of the most powerful tools in the universe. We can use it to our advantage. So, let's.

A classic example of this was a guy at my school. He was King of The World. He wasn't good-looking. He wasn't intelligent. He wasn't polite or overly kind. He wasn't the type to rescue small animals and tend

Man example: you can buy a little silver plate for $200, but the one you hold above your head at Wimbledon means a bit more.

to them in shoeboxes by the heater overnight. He *was* funny, but mostly in a kind of nasty way. In short: he had nothing (other than being first to get a car) that we generally associate with being a 'good' or 'attractive' person. But oh, was he popular. He was adored by all the boys, in both the years above and below him. He was The Guy that all the girls wanted to be with (and, thanks to generosity on his part, most were). He was the guy the teachers let get away with murder.

And why? *Because he believed he was.* There was no overt swaggering or bragging or being a Super Alpha Guy, he just got on with his life knowing that whatever (and indeed whomever) he wanted, he could have. That he was somehow more charmed and lucky and popular than everyone else. And we all believed it. Because he believed it. Unconsciously or otherwise.

If you value yourself highly, others will value you highly, too. If you believe that you attract men without even trying because you're so fuckin' awesome *and how on earth could they resist*, then you will.

It's like being given your own pricing gun at the supermarket.

Note: aiming for a high Perceived Value is not about being selfish or an egocentric maniac. It's about believing you have something of value to offer people: your wit, your warmth, your kindness, your sparkling conversation, your listening skills, your creativity, your ability to make people feel better about themselves when they're feeling like bin sludge, your general gorgeousness and allure. You must believe you're a catch, a winner, an irresistible little muffin dripping with the kind of honey that attracts *all* the bees. Are you sought after? (Yeah!) Should you be? (Yeah!) Then nurture and project an image of self-love, and so it shall be! (Hallelujah!) (Cut to gospel choir.)

THE SECRETY LITTLE TRICK

Instead of wasting energy on worrying if people like you or if men find you attractive, spend energy on making your life as enjoyable, successful and fulfilling as possible. Know your worth at all times. Don't take on other people's projections – that's their stuff.

The more you think about whether people like you, or how men rate you, the more power you're giving to other people. And the more likely you are to be affected if someone doesn't respond to you as you hoped they would. If your expectations are only of yourself and your behaviour, you can maintain them. If they are of other people, you will constantly be disappointed.

By concentrating on improving your own life and developing your self-worth, you become more attractive, more interesting and of 'higher value'. As Sarah Vaughan once sang: 'You're no exception to the rule / I'm irresistible, you fool.'

BEWARE THE BARGAIN BIN

The opposite of **Ms High Perceived Value** is, of course, **Ms Desperado**.

We all know someone who wants so desperately for people to like them, or for people to include them and love them, that all they do is ward everybody off. They *stink* of desperation. (It smells a little like old car batteries and road kill, blended with sulphuric acid and rotting zucchini.)

I have a friend, Ethel, who is gorgeous, smart, owns her own practice and wears fabulous shoes at all times. She ticks all the boxes on the Female Catch form. However . . . whenever we go out, she tries too hard. She latches on to any guy who shows her the smallest amount of interest. Laughs too hard at his jokes. Puts down other women he chats to. Gives him all of her attention for the entire night. Follows him over to his group of friends to re-ignite the conversation. 'Playfully' demands he take her number and call her the next day, unable to hide that she really, really, really wants him to. He can sense what's going on. He knows she has low self-esteem and his perception of her changes from seeing her as a confident woman who cares enough about herself and her friends not to chuck in her night out with them to speak to a guy she just met, to that of a woman who is so keen to meet a man that the rest of her world just falls away once she meets a potential target.

She never understands why he doesn't call her.

Anyone who meets an Ethel immediately picks up on the scent of desperation. It's in their obviously overactive need to be accepted, or do favours, or to make life easier for people living a life they want to be part of. It's in their inability to take a hint that the conversation has wound down. ('So, uh, nice to meet you. I guess I should go and, uh, talk to the host.' '*Great! I'll come.*') It all screams that they would rather go to great lengths to make another person's life more enjoyable than try to improve their own, hoping that this will raise their Perceived Value.

You may think you're *not* Ms Desperado, but if you meet a guy and within a few days you've started revolving your whole existence and timetable around him – sugar, I'm sorry, but you kind of stink.

A woman with a high Perceived Value meets a guy

Perhaps she feels guilty for stealing a 90-year-old woman's name – who knows?

And if Ethel does end up with a guy, since she fell in his lap like a free donut, she's kind of just as disposable.

and gets on with her life. Sure, she's flattered and excited, but she knows that it would be the equivalent of popping herself in the $2 basket to latch onto him without requiring any kind of work from him to secure her. After all, she is very expensive.

So say NO to the bargain bin and YES to the locked glass cabinet (and MAYBE to another serving of ice cream).

Guys will always go for whichever girl projects a higher self-worth, for the same reason people will trample each other to death in the doorway of Myer on Boxing Day – humans like good value. Imagine a guy is presented with two clock radios. The first one is dimly lit, only displays the time it thinks you want to see, and you have to crank it to play the radio, which is the only reason you bought it in the first place. The second one's display comes in three awesome neon colours (one's a new colour scientists didn't even know about), has a surround-sound system, plays a variety of incredible music from around the world, and also has a slurpee machine. Which clock do you want to be? Hint: the second one. (I do realise my hint is actually the answer, but when you go to so much trouble describing a hypothetical piece of electronics, you want it to end well.)

4.

Don't Even Try, Still Get the Guy

*Like fairies, except we won't steal children's teeth.

The fact that there even is an equation for girls means you're ahead of us. We were going to do a secret handshake but couldn't decide on one. We have no plan, we're just kind of out there, floating around. Like jellyfish, but with jeans on.

In this lesson, you'll learn that to attract men, you pretty much need to act as though they don't exist.*

A lot of women are confused. You can't understand why you don't attract men, or attract the wrong kind of men, and why Bernadette from Accounts seems to nail a different guy each week despite the fact that you're definitely hotter. This is partly because you are repeating (usually subconscious) patterns from your previous experiences with men, partly because you don't know how to be a Clever Single Woman (don't worry, you're about to learn) and partly because you have shithouse friends who should be buying you dating books like this for special occasions, instead of flowers or jewellery.

The key to being a Clever Single Woman is in this very simple equation:

**Enjoying Your Life +
Not Looking For a Guy =
A Very Excellent Move.**

ENJOYING YOUR LIFE

The first part – **Enjoying Your Life** – harks back to Lesson 2. People who enjoy their life are a lot more fun to be around. I have a wonderful friend who is a very Clever Single Girl. She blows everyone away, and not because she's the President of the United States or Miss Universe saving orphaned seals, but because she is so active and has such a passion for life. Sure it's annoying trying to fit in a coffee with her, but she'll be inviting you along to her Italian cooking class, or Spanish language lessons, or weekly float tank instead.

Here are some suggestions for positive changes to help you enjoy life:

- Get out more and socialise. Say yes when people invite you along to things, even if it sounds dull, or like they are part of some sicko cult. Just pop on your purple tracksuit and go – Scientology could be awesome, for all you know.

- Actively employ the A Few Quiet Drinks theory. As we all know, the nights when you're dressed like a slob and don't feel like going out, or when you think you're just going out casually for a few quiet drinks, are *always* the ones where you end up dancing to 'Billie Jean' at 3 a.m. and shouting shots of tequila for Fa'Ulongi the bouncer and generally having far more fun than is legal. So, whenever you can sense one of these nights shaping up, don't go home and get changed, don't cancel because there is a high tsunami alert, don't even bother applying eyeliner. Just go and allow chance to run its course. Run, little chance, run!

Receptionist for the Chippendales is going too far, though.

- Consider switching to a job that invigorates and inspires you. As we all know, 86% of relationships begin in the workplace (I made this up). (So do 67% of affairs, but that's for another time). If your work bores you and the people who work there make you envy narcoleptics, you're not very likely to be meet or be introduced to interesting men.
- Engage in a hobby, especially involving group activity. Think more along the lines of trivia nights or personal training, and less along the lines of birdwatching or conspiracy-theory blogging.

NOT LOOKING FOR A GUY

The second part of the equation – **Not Looking For a Guy** – can be a little harder, but is probably more important. The kind of Looking we're trying to stop here involves being too keen to meet or hook up with a guy. Not-Lookingness will become innate when you apply Lessons 1–3 of this Module.

To be fair, it's very easy to fall into the Looking For a Guy trap, especially when you're very newly single, or very tired of being single, or very horny. But remember at all times that looking *does not pay.*

The more you look for something, the less likely it is you will find it. The more you relax and simply believe that it is coming (or is, in fact, already here), and that you needn't be concerned with expending effort to find it, the faster it will find you. It's like when you're crouching down to pick up a hair band and you find that missing earring on your bathroom mat.

When you stop looking, it just pops up by itself.

There's a girl in my extended friendship circle, Odette, and I'm pretty sure you have a friend just like her. She's the one who makes you want to kick furniture even though you love her. She may not be skinny and booby. She may not be classically pretty. In fact she's probably neither of these things. And she probably goes out wearing an ill-fitting bra and the same jeans she has on to grab the papers on a Sunday. But oh, how the men flock to her. They ask for her number. Buy her drinks. Sidle up to her and tell her bad jokes to get a laugh. And the most annoying thing? The thing that hornswoggles you the most? She doesn't even try. IT'S LIKE SHE'S RUBBING YOUR STINKER IN HER NONCHALANCE.   ←

I know, I know, how annoying is she … you wouldn't have her number by any chance, though?

But what's going on is as clear as vodka: *She doesn't look for men, so they look for her.* She's attractive because she doesn't need a guy to confirm to her that she is attractive.

So if you find yourself looking for men who are looking at you, here is what you need to do: STOP. NOW.

Enjoy that you look and feel good and don't worry about how guys respond. Don't worry about getting the attention of the good sort in the blue shirt! Don't bother making eyes at the barman with the floppy hair so that he notices how ravishing you look! Don't waste energy flirting with the guy who fills up your bucket with coins for the pokies! Invest your energy into enjoying yourself instead.

Relevant song lyric: 'There ain't nothing more sexy than a girl who want but don't need me.' ('She Got Her Own', Jamie Foxx)

Irrelevant song lyric: 'Pump up the jam' ('Pump Up the Jam', Technotronic)

Of course you look massively awesome, but the key is to always – *always* – remember you have done all of that for *you*. Not for the benefit of Random Guys. You paid Crystal at NV Hair $210 for you. Bought the dress for you, lengthened your legs with strappy new heels for you, did smoky eye makeup for you. As you're not one of Hugh Hefner's girlfriends, you don't style everything you do for the sole purpose of being attractive to men.

The nanosecond you expect a return on any of these things you do to make yourself look and feel excellent, you pretty much confirm you will not be getting one. Yeah, it bites, but that's the way the daiquiri spills.

It's like that old aphorism: Give to give, not to receive. You give them the visual pleasure of your hotness with no expectation of anything back.

INSIDE A MAN BRAIN

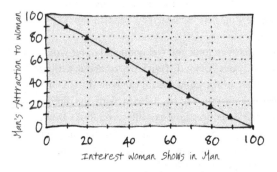

The more intriguing you are vs the less you look at us ... (If you never look at us, we can die, so it gets kind of serious.)

The most perfect (and embarrassingly simple) example of this theory in action is if you have ever seen a mother threaten to leave her toddler in a store because he's not responding to her. She walks out saying, 'Okay, Jeremy, I'll just leave you here and you'll never see mum again. I'm getting in the car', occasionally adding the extra dimension to the charade of producing the car keys and heading for the shop door. Upon seeing this Jeremy freaks out (despite the fact he could have called her bluff by pointing out no one gets their keys out in the shop), thinking that after all these years of believing he could do as he wished because his mother adored him, she was now willing to nonchalantly abandon him and force him to forever live off old chewing gum found under seats and food court scraps. Immediately he rushes to her, fearing it may already be too late. Once he's buried into her waist, mum allows herself a small smile, while everyone else looks on thinking, 'you sucker, Jeremy, you just fell for the oldest trick in the book'. It's exactly the same thing we will fall for today as grown men, only we don't run to our mums (usually).

5.

What Do You Really Want in a Man?

In this lesson, you'll learn that to attract the right man, you need to attract the right man.

A lot of single women sit around in their pyjamas watching re-runs of *Sex & The City*, eating ice-cream and being miserable about the fact that something so important and vital to their happiness is missing from their lives . . . *If only they had bought some chocolate topping,* they think, *then they would be truly, deeply happy.*

But sometimes, *sometimes* their minds shift from their lack of Ice Magic to the fact that it can be so hard finding a good man.

They're all gay, they say. Or married. Or broke and unmotivated. Or too young. Or have too much baggage. Single women spend an enormous amount of ice-cream–fuelled energy thinking about what they *don't* want in a man and what makes a man *unsuitable*. Then they spend energy confirming again and again that there are no good men left.

Good news: Men aren't ice-cream. There's still some left.

DO YOU *KNOW* WHAT YOU WANT?

Come on, be honest. You don't know what you want, do you? You might have a *vague* idea (over the age of 16, owner of a penis*), but have you taken the time to *really* think about what you seek in a man?

*Hopefully an attached penis, otherwise that's Hannibal.

If you were trying to find your dream job, you would have a very clear image in your head of the company, the position and the salary. Why should attracting the kind of man you want be any less calculated? If you don't have a clear idea of the man you want, well I'm not surprised you haven't found him yet.

Creative Visualisation Exercise

Imagine you get into a taxi. The driver, resplendent in his sweat-marked shirt and eau de halitosis, asks you where you would like to go. You tell him your precise destination and he sets off at a pace usually reserved for white vans with flashing lights and red crosses on the side.

But imagine you'd answered, 'Oooh, I don't know . . . I mean, I like the city, but then I also like the beach. Maybe one of the affluent suburbs near the beach is good? Or maybe a trendy inner-city village is better. Oh! I *really* like those pretty tree-lined streets – maybe we could find one of them? And I definitely like parks, so there should definitely be a park in there somewhere . . . No bus stops though. Hate bus stops. Yes, perfect. Head there, thanks.'

The point is that if you don't have a clear vision of what kind of man you want in your life, there is no point even looking. Not being clear about what you want – *exactly what you want* – is like asking the taxi

I don't know, that cab driver sounded okay. He has a job, his own car, a shirt . . .

driver to take you in 89 directions and then getting pissed off when you don't ever arrive. You need to create a clear picture of what you desire in your mind, so that he can fall into your lap – and then you can tell people how it was 'fate' that you wanted to meet a parrot breeder from Brazil with long, shiny dark hair and a PhD in industrial relations and that's who showed up at your door looking for a lost bird.

Unless you stole the bird, that's less fate, more 'crazy'.

The solution lies in learning to harness your **Mega-Powerful *Man*-ifesting Mind Powers™**.

DATING DICTIONARY: MEGA-POWERFUL *MAN*-IFESTING MIND POWERS™

We all have them and they are astonishing and all-powerful. I'm not going to get all hippy tree-huggy on you, but I *am* going to suggest, à la *The Secret*, that you learn the basics of attracting what you want (kind, funny, clever, criminally handsome) over what you don't (unemployed, toothless gambler who wheels trolleys around the streets). What you think about you bring about. You can attract anything you want into your life, even whole complex lists' worth, simply by thinking about it often and believing that it is already yours.

You should know, however, that this works for both the negative and the positive. So, if you constantly think:

- There are no good men out there
- I'll never find a good man
- All the good men are taken

. . . you'll never find a good man. Because there *are* none out there. They *have* all been taken.

Whereas if you think:

- There are wonderful, quality men in abundance, all around me, always
- I attract quality men every day, in every way
- I am grateful and happy that I have attracted the perfect man into my life

. . . and you really *believe* what you are saying, well, your perfect man is yours. Well done!

WHAT HAVE YOU LEARNED?

Now that you know the extent of your Mega-Powerful *Man*-ifesting Mind Powers™, make a list of the key traits you want in a man so that you can mentally lure him into your underground lair. (Obviously, as per Module One, Lesson 2, you will be able to offer him your own pretty impressive list of traits in return.)

Be specific. Take time to REALLY think about what you admire and desire in a partner. Write it down. Imagine him just as you would anything you want (that trip to Italy, that BMW, the health of a family member, toast and jam) so that you can attract him to the point of perfection.

If you have any deal breakers, *make sure you put them in.* A friend, Lola, listed the five traits she wanted in her man, but failed to write down that as she had never wanted children, he would need to be okay with a child-free life. Sure enough, along he came, that 'adventurous tall man with a job in the media', and, oh look . . . his two little boys from his first marriage came too.

There is little point attracting your ambitious, affectionate, generous and loving dolphin trainer if he's

Unless you can train his dolphins to nick his ciggies.

a pack-a-day fagger and you're the president of the National Anti-Smoking Association.

Once you've written your list, keep it in your bedside table drawer and feel happy and excited that somewhere in the world, some wonderful man is already feeling an irresistible urge to come find you.

As a bonus, once you have locked on to the guy you want, it will have the added effect of stopping you sending signals to duds. In fact, you might say this method is exactly like installing a DudFilter 3000 in your life, except you wouldn't say that, because it's a made-up product and you'd look silly. But take it from me, right now there are millions of dud guys about to come in contact with you.

6.

Let Men Chase You

In this lesson, you'll learn that you must allow men to pursue you – and never the other way around. Although completely counter to your self-image as a powerful woman, playing cat and mouse is critical to romantic success. *Monopoly*, less so.

You know, we've got a lot in common. Just like you're doing right now, I got some great advice from a book. When I was freshly (read: messily) single and working at *Cosmopolitan* magazine – a magazine where there is a whole room dedicated to books on relationships, diets and new sex positions from Uruguay – the hard-line dating book *The Rules*, by two moxie-brimming birds from New York, quite literally fell off the shelf into my hands.

The Rules isn't for everyone – some friends I later recommended it to thought it was complete bullshit, full of childish head games and *Stepford Wives*-style brainwashing – but for me, at a time when I was trying to get a grip, it was brilliant. I felt like some kind of Transformer, but instead of morphing into a

True. Although we do like getting $200 for walking around the block.

semitrailer, I morphed into a strong, happy woman who had 'reclaimed her confidence'. (I know, vomit.)

The standout revelation was its emphasis on the psychology of the unobtainable, summed up by these fundamentals:

Men like to hunt.
Men like to chase.
Men like to conquer.

This does not make men Neanderthal brutes. It doesn't make them bad. It just makes them male. And being male means they like to make the first move (or at least think they did), and to continue making the moves until they have 'won' you. Whether it's fuelled by the twin-engines of biology and thousands of years of patriarchal imprinting, or whether men just use this biology stuff as an excuse, who can say?

Either way:

- Men get a thrill from chasing and (eventually) winning women over.
- Men don't want women to chase them.
- Men only chase if they're genuinely interested in the win.
- Men don't want the chase to be too easy.
- Men will sometimes piss off once the chase is over, which is why it cannot be made too easy for them.

Jesus, even Paris Hilton knows this: 'If you give it up to a guy, he won't respect you. He'll want you much more if he can't have you.' (I promise this is the only time Paris Hilton will be used as a pillar of good advice in this book.)

Sure, some men can't be arsed and will instead go

[Handwritten margin note, left:] Totally true. If I clear my mind, I can hear very softly the words, 'hunt, chase, conquer' being chanted in my head. I originally misheard this as 'rum, shake, conga' and led a few unfulfilled years.

[Handwritten margin note, left lower:] It's like throwing a stick at a dog's feet.

for the easy kill (technical term: One-Night Stand). But even with an easy kill there is still a 'hunt' . . . it's just that it only lasts for three hours. There will always be the guy who at 8.30 p.m. is showering you with compliments and cocktails, but when he senses you're not going to bed with him that night, he pulls a Houdini. At 11 p.m., when you and your girl-friends are moving on to the next bar, you see him making out with a girl on the street, hailing a cab while groping her arse. (**Please note:** Women are absolutely guilty of the same behaviour: We're more than capable of flirting feverishly and then heading home with a different man whose last name we are yet to learn.)

In this case, it's not even an easy kill – that gazelle was already half dead.

But there's no arguing with the fact that most men are hunters and they desire that which doesn't come easily to them.

I can hear your brain spinning in disgust and offence. *Calm the hell down.* The fact men like to hunt and chase does not immediately infer that:

- we're little cavewomen who just sit there, dividing berries into edibles and poisons, waiting for men to come along and belt us with a club and drag us into a cave; or that

If they do, give them a poison one.

- we're giving up any of our power or equality by choosing to allow them to chase us; or that
- we must necessarily give in to their competitive inclinations.

All it means is that we know it's human nature to want what isn't readily available – and for men, without this tension, there's nothing to 'conquer'.

No one was itching to be the first guy to get to the bottom of Mt Everest.

WHAT HAVE YOU LEARNED?

All men like to chase. Your dad chased your mum. Your brother chased his wife. Barney chased Wilma. Edward chased Bella. Alexander chased Tatiana. Barack chased Michelle. Also, remember that a lot of men, especially those flirting with metrosexuality, don't know or admit they like The Chase, *but they do*.

My advice is to be prepared for The Chase. *Always*. After a while, you won't even realise you're doing it. Just like that thing you do when you put your hair behind your ear when you're nervous. It's adorable, by the way. Keep doing it.

We may have got snazzier pants in the last few thousand years, and ditched cave walls for tablet laptops, but the caveman is alive and well in all men. The thrill of the hunt has gone from most of our lives (KFC is significantly easier to catch than mammoth), but if anything that makes the thrill even more addictive in the one area the hunt still exists – women. And Zoë's dead right – we don't want it to be too easy. Have you ever seen what happens at the greyhound races when the dogs catch the bunny? After a few seconds they all just get bored and wander off looking for something better.

So to recap: our psyches lie somewhere between Neanderthal Man and a fast dog. This has <u>not</u> been a positive chapter for the male ego.

7.

The Chase Commandments

In this lesson, you'll learn the foundations of The Chase. (We really should have made you work a little harder for it, to be honest.)

The Chase needn't be demeaning,* it needn't be contrived, and it needn't feel fake. If you're genuinely enjoying and loving yourself and your life, The Chase happens without you even realising it. You're going about your life, you're feeling great, you have a high Perceived Value and you have an expectation that a man has to show you he's worthy of your attention before you fall at his feet and start obsessing over his text messages. And so The Chase begins. Here are the Ten Commandments for negotiating it successfully.

*Nor should it have the Benny Hill music playing – it's more serious than that.

1. If You Don't Believe You're Worth Chasing, You'll Never Be Chased

Ensure you have installed your confidence chip before you start, because playing The Chase without a healthy amount of genuine, concrete confidence is like trying to beat Tiger Woods at golf, blindfolded and with a teaspoon. If you don't think that men should be chasing you because you're not worthy, then they won't. And if for some reason they do, you will either fail at The Chase, and/or (consciously or otherwise) push them away with your insecurities or feelings of worthlessness. The Chase also demands patience and respect: respect for yourself and respect for the game.

Also, respect for Aretha Franklin, once you find out what it means to her. →

2. The Less Effort You Make, the More He Will Make

Don't try to chat him up. Don't ask him for his number. Don't slip him your card as he's leaving. Don't Facebook him. To smile and be delightful is your only role. A truly attractive woman never has to hunt. She can sit completely mute at a bar with a smile, and men will gravitate towards her like emos to black hair dye.*

* or even like emos to a black hole (that's right, not even emos can escape their gravitational pull).

3. Be a Challenge

So, tell me. Exactly how turned on are you by a guy who drops everything for you, calls, texts and emails you constantly, is *always* available and is altogether too keen. (If the answer is 'a lot', you're not looking for a relationship, you're looking for a pet.) I think it's fair to assume that most of us don't find this behaviour to be very attractive. Why? Because it all comes too easily! It's no fun! It's, well, *strange!* Remember: humans are wired to value things that offer a challenge more. This is why we climb enormous mountains that kill us, run marathons, buy shoes we can't afford and secretly hanker for Bad Boys.

4. Be Strong and Have Faith

I won't lie to you (you'd only resent me later). The Chase can be hard. It can be frustrating and torturous, and feel like you are going against every fibre in your body. Despite it being an extremely primitive notion, it feels exceptionally unnatural. You'll feel silly, like you're playing games and you're 'better than this'. But remember: it takes a woman of extreme self-confidence and grace to allow a man to chase her. There's not a lot 'better' than that.

If you're finding it hard, just know that it's killing us too. But if you stop, all the excitement goes. Like juggling.

5. Treat Guys You Like As Though They're Guys You Don't Like

If you ignore every other one of these commandments (fool!), don't ignore this one. Equal parts simple and profound, this gem is a whopping great smack in the face when you're having trouble with a guy you REALLY like. When you're flipping out because he's not responding as he's 'supposed' to, or at the very least, as you wish he would. *Think of him as a guy you don't like, and treat him like one.* After all, it's the ones we *don't* like who always pursue us so fiercely, who don't give up, who call and text when they say they will. And why? Because we get on with our fun, exciting, fulfilling lives instead of thinking about them obsessively. And, trust me, that's the most powerful aphrodisiac in Aphrodisiaville.

Equal parts simple and profound for you; equal parts infuriating and Crisis Meeting at the Pub for us. It really works.

6. If He's Not Interested, It's a Blessing

If he's not chasing you, and you're doing Everything Right, that is totally okay. You should expect this – it will happen. For despite your feminine allure, there will be men who just aren't up to the challenge or The Chase. This is because they're not interested, they're not available, or they're not confident enough to think they deserve you. This is a GREAT THING, because if he doesn't have the energy or desire to chase, the relationship will never succeed anyway. (Feel free to punch the air as you think of all the heartache and headfuck you just saved yourself.)

Common reasons for not chasing include:

- He's not attracted to you. (Hard to believe, but unbelievably this happens on occasion.)
- He's not available, either mentally or literally (girlfriend, fiancée, wife, boyfriend, 56 kilos of baggage from a fresh break-up, family pet on deathbed).
- He's not confident enough to approach you or to indicate his interest. (Which means you don't want him anyway. Sure, shy men seem adorable at first, but 'shy' is really just code for deeply self-conscious, or possessing low self-esteem.)
- He's a hologram caused by the reflection of your martini glass against the beer taps on the bar.

7. You Can't Behave in Courting As You Do in Business

Hey, I know you're a successful, powerful, amazing female. I know you decide what you want and you go for it – and that you usually get it. I know you're a BA PhD MBA CEO MD and that your response to being presented with a challenge is to attack it, like squishing an infant fly on your desk.

But this does not translate to The Chase, or courting in general. Never has, never will. The delicate initial stages of a relationship require a soft approach – The Chase demands a willingness to accept you will not be in charge; it will not always go your way. You cannot orchestrate this as you do your career. Be at peace with this. It is what it is. And it is okay.

Although you can have company picnics – they're called 'dates'.

8. Easy Come, Easy Go

What is easily won is easily lost. Take the man who bamboozles you very, very quickly with adoration and affection and dates and gifts (Easy Come). Either he'll wear himself out (read: dump you) once you give in to his charm, or you'll tire of his OTT ways and start ignoring his calls (Easy Go). Alternatively, if you give yourself to a guy (emotionally, physically, etc.) too quickly (Easy Come), he won't value you, and will eventually go off to find another challenge elsewhere (Easy Go). The common ground here, of course, is that if something comes too easily, it will often leave with a similar pace and effortlessness. (Just like finding $100 at an ATM. Or a free beer.)

9. Let Him Assume the Reins

This one is a toughie. But as Toni Braxton once wisely said, 'Let go, let it flow, let it flow, let it flow'. Being chased is a wonderful thing, for lots of reasons. Obviously, there is the ego side of things – someone is attracted to you enough to try to woo you – but the less we serve and honour the ego, the better. (Recommended reading: *A New Earth*, by Eckhart Tolle.) No, what is most delightful about being chased is that it is you *allowing* something to happen as opposed to you trying to *make* something happen. When you allow him to take the reins – deciding where to go for that coffee, which wine you'll drink with dinner, which stackhat you'll wear when he picks you up on his BMX – you let him shine. And you enable him to show you how he thinks you deserve to be treated. Men revel in this because it allows them to show off their Best Possible Self, and to prove to you how awesome a guy they are. It's tremendously confidence-boosting for them. All you have to do for, say, the first five dates, is to look and feel your best, be excellent company (e.g. your usual sparky self) and be appreciative. Hell, I'd date you if you did all that*.

Author is lying. She is obviously already in a serious relationship with George Clooney.

10. Actions Speak Louder Than Words (especially in a game of Charades)

Even the Three Wise Men chased a star. (Idiots. It was light years away ... AND in a vacuum ... AND very hot once you actually reached it.)

Sure, this whole Chase thing isn't a new concept. Even men have heard of it. And many men know that they have a better chance if they even create the *illusion* of a chase. So make sure you can distinguish a man with alluring words from a man who actually follows though. This means being brutally honest with yourself about his behaviour. If a man chases you, and insists on locking you down for a date even if you tell him you're busy for four of the nights he suggests, he is investing in you. If he emails you for a date and then doesn't follow up for three days, he is not investing in you. Listen to his actions, not his words. (Especially if they come in the shape of 11 p.m. Friday night texts.)

To cut a long story short, we are the eager puppy itching to have you make us fetch a stick. We don't want you to put the stick in our mouths, we want to see it fly out ahead of us, beating us for a bit, before we triumphantly pounce on it and trot back in all our glory, proclaiming to you with a proud glance that yes, we were able to catch a stick. We are masters of the world.

I realise I've once again used dogs as an analogy for guys. Please keep reading to find out how to make guys stop peeing on trees and humping your leg. (Of course, I'm kidding. That's impossible.)

8.

Never, Ever Make the First Move

In this lesson, you'll learn the art of allowing men to initiate interaction. You'll also learn that you pretty much seal the doom of your entire relationship just by disobeying this one simple rule.

> *'I wish more women would make the first move.'*
> – David, 32, lawyer

> *'Why should we always have to make the first move?'*
> – Cameron, 25, model

'what, I don't get asked for quotes in the book?'
– Hamish, scribble guy

> *'Women want equality – well, why they can't they ask us out for dates, then?'*
> – Steven, 32, engineer

As the dating columnist for *Cosmopolitan*, I have undertaken to ask pretty much every man I meet, single or in relationships, their thoughts on this topic. Amazingly, many of them, like David, Cameron and Steven, will sit there, look me dead in the eye and tell me lies.

And they are *lies*. Because deep down no man actually wants a woman to hit on him. Let me rephrase that. No man looking for a Quality Relationship wants a woman to hit on him. Those just looking for a 'good time' have no qualms about it whatsoever. But we're not concerned with that lot, as fun as they are.

So, guys say they're tired of doing all the work. Tired of the possibility of rejection every time they spot a lady of interest. They're shy. They want some help to get the ball rolling, to know that the girl is interested.

we're only saying that for the same reason we want someone to make the 'couch-toilet' – we're slack.

But when a girl actually does this, when she flirts openly with a guy, starts the conversation, slips him her number, there is a small part of him that dies inside. It's not his ego. Nor is it his masculinity. It's his *need to put in effort*. Y'see, when you do these things, he immediately knows you're keen, which means he needn't spend weeks or months trying to ascertain whether you are or not. You deprive him of The Chase.

Once he's put your number into his phone and you've sashayed away thinking about what an exciting New Generation bird you are, he's looking at the fun girl by the door who has paid him absolutely no attention all evening. Because whereas you have offered your intentions on a platter, she has offered him a challenge.

As one guy I asked put it, if she immediately makes her intentions transparent, he pretty much allocates her to 'disposable' status. He doesn't believe women *can't* let guys know they're keen, but that there is a way to do it that is encouraging but still tinged with a little mystery. 'You want to feel like you had something to do with attracting her,' he said, 'that you had to earn her interest as opposed to being a target in her trajectory.'

It's not about sitting back on your Snow Queen throne in your fancy uggboots, swizzling your icy beverage, waiting for a guy to bow down to you and beg for a date, risking rejection, belittling and much ribbing from his friends. **No.** It's about allowing a guy to show you he's interested, which in my opinion and experience, is going to create a far more harmonious and enjoyable situation/relationship for both parties.

If you're thinking it's possible to 'set it up' so that he makes the first move, I don't recommend it. Subtle encouragement is more than enough. We don't need to fish or hint or actively invite men to be interested in us: they either are or they're not. Just as it is with us and men. Encouragement can be as simple as a dazzling smile when he's looking your way, and then that delightful little thing you do where you catch his eye then look down just he returns the gaze. This way, he knows he's walking into safe territory, as opposed to walking up to a woman who is likely to verbally submerge his confidence into a large vat of boiling lard.

Even if women *do* try to make the first move, most of the time it fails. Men and women are vastly different when it comes to communicating. Some women might *think* they are making the first move, visually or verbally, but just as hints about anniversaries and Prada wallets for birthday presents go unnoticed, so too do many female 'pick-up' signals and lines. (T-shirts with 'I have breasts and I'm single!' emblazoned across the front excluded.)

But if you're determined, and somehow you *do*

'As Confucius said: 'The free cheeseburger can never taste as juicy as the burger purchased through a day's labour.'
(John Confucius, that is. I went to high school with him. Smart guy.)

Don't bother. We imagine all girls to be wearing that T-shirt all the time anyway.

Guys have two similarly sized parts in their brain: Laziness and Desire to Conquer. The second is only slightly bigger, so sometimes we're happy to let the first bit run things ... and let you make the first move.

start off the relationship by making the first move, subconsciously you have created a template where you'll now be expected to initiate everything throughout the entire relationship. If you think you can ask him out on the first date and then sit back and enjoy him wooing and courting you, you're mistaken, and have obviously NOT BEEN PAYING ATTENTIONS.

Of course, there are women who genuinely don't want a 'chaser', and would prefer a less aggressive man. For them, making the first move makes sense because it immediately sets up the dynamic of the relationship. If that works for you, congratulations! You can stop reading and enjoy life with your new friend. But most of us are looking for something a little more challenging, a little more equal.

The fact is, successful male–female relationships begin naturally with the man falling for and pursuing the woman. The woman feels adored and cherished from day one and the man feels proud of his securing her. This foundation – where both parties are equally thrilled about their entry into the relationship – solves a great many possible relationship issues. How much more secure, for example, will *you* feel knowing your guy chased you and wouldn't take no for an answer, as opposed to knowing you asked him out, and he didn't have to invest any effort or expose himself to any vulnerability to land you?

The answer is 60. you will feel '60 more secure'. We researched it.

COMPREHENSION EXERCISE

When a guy says: 'I want women to ask me out.'
What he's really saying is: 'Golly, am I confused! I actually don't want that at all. If a woman asks me

out, I question her motives and her level of aggressiveness. Is she going to be better at me in poker, too?'

Almost, but we never say 'golly'.

When a girl says: 'I make the first move because I don't like to sit around and wait for someone to pick me out. It's the 21st century, for God's sake.'
What she's really saying is: 'I'm currently unaware that my philosophy on life doesn't translate to relationships. I'll learn this the hard way, unfortunately, when I call men and then later berate myself for it when they don't call back or fail to lock in dates even after I put myself out there like that.'

When a guy says: 'I don't play games.'
What he's really saying is: 'The need for games and challenges is so deeply entrenched into me, via societal conditioning and biological hardwiring, that I'm actually unaware of how much I not only play them, but revel in them.'

In fact, saying 'I don't play games' is one of our best game moves. We're crafty like that. If by 'crafty' you mean 'kind of a liar'.

When a girl says: 'I don't care about being chased and all that bullshit.'
What she's really saying is: 'I believe this intellectually, but *emotionally*, when he doesn't call after he says he will, and never thinks he has to treat me to a proper date, and never feels like he has to commit to me because it is a given that I'll be around, I will feel the hurt.'

FIELD REPORT

I was at a launch for a new toe shampoo or some such thing a few years ago and noticed a guy standing across the room from me. He was pretty good-looking, if by 'pretty', you mean 'devastatingly'. I tried to catch his eye (–6 points) and was disappointed when he didn't take the bait. My girlfriend saw what was happening – or the small river of drool pooling in the corner of my mouth, I can't remember which – and suggested I go talk to him (–17 points.) I guffawed and carried on a bit, because I knew from all my past experiences that making the first move spelled doom (+10 points). After an hour of me surreptitiously thieving glances (–5 points), my girlfriend had had enough. So she wrote my number on her business card and stomped over to give it to him (–5897 points).

I remember watching it all go down: her smiling and pointing me out across the room, me dropping my head in embarrassment and distress, him looking bemused by the whole situation. She bounced back, thrilled with the fact that she had saved this man from leaving my life forever. On one level, I was a little bit happy and relieved – I wanted to meet this man with every hair in my nostril – but on another, I was pissed off that I had just been forced into doing something that I so fervently opposed: *making the first move*.

What happened next was textbook stuff. (Rather like this book, but without the awesome pie charts.) There were a few days of my poor, well-meaning friend listening to me say, 'SEE? I TOLD YOU you shouldn't have given him my number! I bet he has a girlfriend and now I look like a complete desperado'. Then he called me on a private number.

I giggled and told him it was my friend's idea to give him my number, but we both saw through my thinly-veiled attempt at pretending it was all out of my hands – *I* had made the first move. After four and a half minutes of stilted, awkward conversation, he said something to the effect of, 'So, I guess I should be asking you out for a coffee or something, right?'.

'YES!', one side of me screamed, *because you're so obscenely attractive!*

'NO!', another side of me screamed, *because you just said, 'I guess I should', which implies obligation, not infatuation!*

'MAYBE!', my remaining side screamed (I am an isosceles triangle), *but I'd really prefer a chai latte if that's okay, as coffee upsets my stomach!*

I agreed, reprimanding myself for the self-flagellation. He said, 'Okay, how about Saturday?', before launching that great Dating Get Out of Jail Free card, 'I'll text you'.

He didn't text, there was no coffee (*or* chai latte) and my point was proven again. He did actually call a week or so later, mumbling some shitty excuse and serving up the vague promise of another attempt, but I saved us both the bother of keeping up the façade and deleted both his message and his number.

The moral of the story is: this is a *boring* story. A repeat lesson-learner. I forced something onto someone who didn't want to do it off their own bat – not a very happy situation.

So much for Scenario 1 (reality). Let's rewind time and imagine (and women's imaginations are never more active than when there is a fresh man in the fold) how things *might* have gone with me and Mr I'll Text You.

Scenario 2: We exchange glances a few times at the party, I enjoy his visual candy, and when he leaves without finding a way to talk to me or ask for my number, I say some words more suited to a pirate ship than a lovely book like this, but get over it in a day or two because I know that: a) Lady Fate will step in if we're meant to meet again; b) He was unavailable or not attracted to me, and this is fine, because mum told me I'm pretty and she's always right; and c) I did the right thing.

Scenario 3: We exchange glances a few times at the party, I enjoy his visual candy, and before I know it, he's standing next to me at the bar, making small talk about the fact that the cocktails are blue, which is odd given that blue isn't a fruit. I, of course, refer him to the blueberry and its lesser known, but no less important cousin, the quandong. He smiles and obviously somewhere inside his brain decides I should be his wife. We chat some more, I say that unfortunately I have to leave, and he asks for my number. He calls the next day and asks me to dinner the following night. (Not to 'hang out', not for coffee – dinner. Impressive.) I say I'd love to but I'm busy. He says, 'Wednesday?'. I make a sound that sounds *terribly* apologetic and say I'm busy that night also. He says, 'Thursday?', and I laugh and say, 'Why, that would be lovely'. I get off the phone feeling pretty special indeed. Because it's nice to be pursued, isn't it?

Scenario 4: We exchange glances a few times at the party, I enjoy his visual candy, and after a little while he walks over, smiles, looks me up and down and says, 'Honey? You are fittin' the *shit* out of that dress. Oh. My. God. Allow me to introduce myself. I'm Glen and this is my boyfriend Terrence, and we just *had* to come and say hi.' And we have a wonderful conversation and laugh a lot, then drink seven blue cocktails each and go dancing, and I end up trying not to vomit up my canapés in the cab on the way home at 2.16 a.m.

Scenario 5: He's a werewolf. He eats you. (This is why I'm not allowed to do the 'scenario' bits.)

PERCENTAGE OF MEN WHO PREFER TO MAKE THE FIRST MOVE

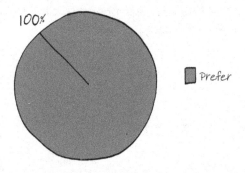

100%

☐ Prefer

WHAT HAVE YOU LEARNED?

In Eastern philosophy, Yin is perceived to be the feminine energy, Yang the masculine. Yin is pull; Yang is push. So be calm and receive the energy, rather than trying to create it. Also, try to remember that every little thing happens for a reason. Don't fuck with the universe's Grand Plan. Guys will get your contact details if they want them. You don't need to help them along.

what zoë calls 'the universe' is actually an equally massive thing (but with fewer spaceships flying round it) — and that is, a guy's desire to get what he wants. If we really want something bad enough, we'll always find a way to make it happen (driving a car on the moon is a fairly good example). In fact, if you try to help us, it takes us back to childhood memories of mum insisting on helping us ride our first skateboard, hence taking away any sense of achievement, then we lose self-confidence, then David Simmons punches us and takes our Ninja Turtle. See how quickly things can spin out of control? Scary, I know.

9.

You Control the Pace of the Relationship

In this lesson, we'll demonstrate how the woman needs to keep her foot on the brake pedal in the early stages of courtship.

One of the fundamental laws of courtship is this: **men will always try to speed things up and women will always need to slow them down.**

We saw it with the boy next door who didn't hesitate to show us his so we would show him ours. We saw it with the grotty, grimy-pawed little boys in Year 9 who tried to sweet-talk us into making out with them so they could get a grope. We saw it with the sweaty 17-year-olds who fetched us beers all night at a party so they could launch into some high-intensity frottage in the hallway without resistance. We saw it with the guy we dated for a few weeks who produced a ring made of grass to get us into the sack. And as grown-up women, we see it when the guy we pashed on the dance floor on a Saturday night calls and texts on the Sunday for a movie that night.

To many women this is attractive, because it feels

I promise you, though: your guy will be very passionate about getting an in-car DVD player. which I firmly support.

without wanting to invoke phallic images, the mentality is something similar to that of a battering ram.

like the guy is so into you that he simply cannot wait to lock you down. And sometimes it is attractive. But that still doesn't mean you should allow him to dictate how quickly this happens.

A man who has decided you're a fantastic bird and worth pursuing will always try to hurry things along, to secure the win as fast as possible. Whether this is your phone number, your body or your undivided monogamous attentions, subconsciously, at every stage of attraction and dating, each thing you stand to offer them equals a small mountain to conquer.

This impulse to fast-track is bad for three reasons:

1. Courting is the most delightful part of a relationship. Why let it collapse within ten days?
2. When humans win the prize too quickly or easily, the prize no longer interests them.
3. You need time to figure out if he is worth investing in, and so does he, in you.

It's like how excited you used to get about your birthday when you were little. All you can think and talk and dream about is the day, the wonderful day when all your friends come over and you eat sugar in various solid and liquid forms, and you get shitloads of presents. You're so consumed with the day that life leading up to it becomes a blur. You're not aware of what you're doing, and you don't care, because there is Something Exciting in sight. But once that birthday has passed, and you're sitting alone in your empty house, you feel so incredibly low. Sure, you've got all your presents and you had your adoration and glycation, but now you're not sure what there is to keep living for in a pin-the-tail-on-the-donkey–free world.

A lot of it is from the sugar crash, but some of the emptiness is genuine.

And this is how it can be for men.

You are the birthday party. Winning you over is the goal, and when the lead-up is in motion, he's not thinking straight. He just wants more, more, more, until he gets the prize. He'll want to see you every day, twice a day. Forget going to the pub with Wazza and Gazza, he'd rather drink unpronounceable wine on a picnic rug with you.

I have a friend, Winnie, who is a chronic Relationship Accelerator. It used to kill me to see her going out four nights in one week with a guy she'd just met. She's a Life's Too Short girl: she thinks because she's in her thirties she doesn't have time to play games and that rules are for losers, and she'll probably never read this book. Recently, I caught up with her to discover that she was in love. 'I asked *him* out,' she told me smugly, 'and I see him and call him whenever I like.' She stopped just short of poking her tongue out at me and saying, 'See? You CAN ask a guy out and it work'.

Cut to three months later: they've split and she's a mess. 'He just wanted out,' she said. And I desperately felt for her. Her behaviour is representative of so many women I meet: they feel love should be spontaneous and free-flowing. That your feelings should be in charge. That your heart should lead the way. She often says, 'If I wait a week between dates, I'll lose all momentum', which is absolutely normal to *feel*, but not necessarily advantageous to *act out*. Good things *do* come to those who wait.

DATING DICTIONARY: LIMERENCE

A scientific term for the initial feelings of attraction

The romantic part is, he'll be getting hassled by Warwick and Gareth (Wazza and Gazza) about this, but will still persist.

Like when you think it's a good idea to dress as Batman, but then when you act it out the priest is all like, 'you have to leave sir, you weren't invited to this wedding'.

between two people. The guy you've fallen for is known as the 'limerent object' – and your emotions and feelings become dependent on this object. If he calls, you're wildly happy. If he doesn't, you're tremendously pissed off. **It's not a logical or rational state of mind.** Limerence is the reason people believe in love at first sight, the reason they start affairs, the reason they leave their partners and children and run away with 22-year-olds. It's basically a form of irrational obsession, thinly veiled in the cloak of 'love'. And it's *very* useful to remember the effects of limerence next time you decide you can *totally* see him whenever he wants to see you and that there will be no long-term consequences to your relationship. Because when you are focused on your limerent object, *you're not thinking straight.* You're thinking bendy.

Here is what you must do: Step in, play policewoman and slow him down. Even if you're loving, nay, *inhaling* the frenetic, lusty pace, and want to see him eight days out of seven, you *must* slow it down.

These early days are a time to be enjoyed and cherished. A time to get to know each other, bit by bit, story by story. (This is especially crucial, since on a single date we tend to pretty much go over our entire lives – well, the impressive parts, anyway. The bits about how you still sleep with a night light on and have 'issues' with body hair strangely don't get a mention.) Rushing through all of this because he, or you, or both of you, simply want to (or more accurately, your hormones want to), doesn't mean you should. For the benefit of both of you, and the potential relationship, the longer you can hold him back from bursting across the finish line of knowing he 'has' you, the better.

There is a chance you will also want to write him limericks, but that is coincidental, and not what the word means.

Having plans in place and him swooping in at the last moment with new ones is a brilliant situation in which to set the pace and define your boundaries. Remember: a lady should always control and monitor the pace of a relationship, and that pace should be set to about 5km/h. It's your car and you're the driver. With you at the wheel, you're in a position to create a fantastic, strong foundation for your relationship.

Knowing how to pump the brakes is a skill and if you develop it properly from the outset it will serve you well, not only throughout courting and dating, but also in relationships and marriage (more on that later).

A Good Man will be cool with you wanting to slow things down. He'll appreciate and respect that you may not want to see him more than three times a week for the first month, or not sleep with him till the fifth date. A Not Good Man (didn't say Bad . . .) will insist the pace remains set to the tempo of the person with the testicles, and will make you feel uneasy or silly about pulling up the reins. What men should realise is that you're actually doing them a favour by pumping the brakes. You're prolonging the attraction, the fun and the excitement and, most importantly, providing them with – you guessed it – a challenge.

Men Can Be Bunny Boilers Too!

Ominously (cue Gothic organ music), wanting to bowl you into a relationship too quickly can be a massively unsavoury hint of things to come. It's not cute, it's actually unhealthy for a man to start calling you eighteen times a day, asking you out every night and

It is roughly the jogging pace he should be able to keep up beside your car if you're driving from the Gold Coast to Melbourne.

I actually guessed hotdog, but 'challenge' is better. We love those. (Even more than hotdogs.)

showering you with gifts and full-on texts. And imagine what a man would say about a woman showing this behaviour! Psycho, bunny-boiler, crazy, etc. So why shouldn't it be seen as equally unstable when a man does it? It should.

Too much way too soon can be a sign of the emotionally unstable. Some men will shepherd women into a relationship before the woman has a chance to think about whether it's what she wants, or if she's comfortable with the intensity level. Some men do this deliberately so that you begin to distance yourself from your family and social life, and before you know it you're feeling trapped with a man who is dominant, controlling or overprotective. This is BAD. Not romantic. Bad.

This is the equivalent of being tricked into the passenger seat of the car with promises of Disneyland, only to find out you're going to the steam train museum. I hate the steam train museum.

TAKE A TEST

Which response indicates a Good Guy?
On Wednesday afternoon he asks to see you Friday night. You politely decline. He says:
A. 'Of course, you have already booked in dinner with the girls. No dramas. So . . . how about Saturday, then?'
B. 'But Friday's the only night I can see you! Can you change it so that I can steal you Friday and they have you Saturday?'
C. 'S'up to you. Opportunity doesn't knock twice, baby.'

You have to cancel a movie because your best friend just broke up with her man and she's desolate. He says:
A. 'Is she okay? Do you need a lift over there?'

B. 'What time will you be done? We can still probably make the later session.'

C. 'Well, she *is* a bit of a slut . . .'

You had a great date with him last night and he's calling for another tonight. You tell him you have work to do. (You don't, of course – you're just pumping the brakes.) He says:

A. 'Ah, you do love torturing me, don't you? I'll get you back for this one day.'

B. 'Why not just do it now and then I can see you tonight? Simple!'

C. 'Buuuuullshit. See you at 7.' [Click.]

ANSWERS

I know, I know, obviously the winner is Guy C. He's honest, upfront and persistent and clearly has access to some of the finest crack available. But seriously, we all know it's A, and we all know why: he is respectful enough to actually LISTEN to what you have told him and then respond accordingly, and not to try to change your mind because what *he* wants is more important. Finally, he accepts your decision with good grace and enthusiastically asks for another option. Remember that you're not doing anything wrong by politely declining seeing him. Nothing at all. What a catch Guy A is. Send him my way if you ever find him. ⟵

Sadly, B is probably the most common of the three kinds of responses. This kind of guy confuses being pushy with being romantic, and will not settle for you having plans already in place, or things popping up to change pre-made plans the two of you have made, because he is on a Romance Trajectory, and dammit,

[handwritten margin note:] Don't keep him for yourself. Zoë has to learn if she's going to give you this advice, she can't just come in and steal the guy once you get him. *Bad* Zoë.

you WILL be wooed. He's the same guy who will invite you along to everything for the first month, and then pull back and start wanting Guy Time as soon as you genuinely want to accompany him. He's the same guy who will gently force you into staying over at his place when you *really* don't want to – because you have no clothes for the next day and have to be at a meeting at 8 a.m. – by saying you're not 'spontaneous' enough, or you're boring, or unadventurous, or blahblahblah. (And he's the same guy who will become ever so subtly less interested in you once you allow the P into the V.* Sorry.)

*Then he will swiftly go to S and F. ('Sleep' and 'Fart' that is, not 'Siberia' and 'Fandango'.)

There is a fourth kind: Option D (D for 'Delete From Phone'). This is the guy who, when told you're busy and can't see him Friday night, says: 'Okay, cool. Well, maybe another time. Have fun.' And you never hear from him again. Or if you do, it's 9.08 p.m. on a Friday night and he's asking if you're out tonight. This guy's a chump and you mustn't waste any more time on him than it has taken me to write this sentence. He's about as good for you as drinking a cyanide milkshake on a busy highway. He senses that you're going to be Hard Work and he throws in the towel straight away. This isn't the kind of man you want to date, or love, or marry. He's either Just Not That Into You (see Reading List, p.253), or he has sensed that you're actually a top bird worthy of a good solid chase, but he's simply not up for that at this time in his life. That's okay. Let him go. Accept that every guy comes into your life for a reason, and this guy exists to teach you to have the strength to simply let him go without a fight, or a sleepless night, or an atomic bitch about him with Trace, Deb and Shezzy.

In short, he's a scavenger, and you deserve better than being treated like a carcass. You have better shoes for a start.

WHAT HAVE YOU LEARNED?

Pacing the courting and dating stages of the relationship benefits both of you. First up, it allows you a chance to create boundaries (even if they're frustrating and go against your natural urges) about how you won't drop everything for him just because he wants you to. (And even though he thinks he wants you to, he actually, absolutely does NOT want you to.) Second, he gets to enjoy his 'mission' for longer, instead of it coming too easily and bringing the risk of an unappreciated victory. And finally, *you* get to enjoy more of that delirious deliciousness that is courtship, as well as getting to suss out if he's genuinely interested in you (and thus willing to sit tight if you do pump your brakes), or if he's going to bail the second it becomes too hard. Win-dingin-win.

Again, giving in to our demands is exactly what we do not want, despite the fact we're making the demands in the first place (and we thought you were confusing). This is the key to understanding the male brain. Nothing bores us faster than getting our goal too easily, or in this case, too swiftly. It would be no fun winning the World Cup if the other team all fainted and you just got to kick unopposed goals for 90 minutes. It'd be weird, sure — certainly one of the more talked about World Cup finals — but it would be worse than losing, because you won it too quickly and too easily.

10.

Ignore People Who Say, 'Life's Too Short to Play Games', Because They Are Morons

In this lesson, you'll learn why all of this Chase stuff is so important and why those who say it's bullshit are generally those who need to do it the most.

At least half of my friends think that my theories on love are violently flawed. One of them, Maggie, tells me it's all games. Childish. That you can't possibly hope to keep up the façade once you're living together or married. You've got to have balls, she says. If you want something, you have to grab it. I'm graceful enough not to point out her audacity in saying this as a single woman in her mid 30s who can't find the relationship she's looking for.

Alas, for every self-confident fox who administers The Chase there is a woman standing next to her, rolling her eyes, making tsk-tsk noises and saying: 'Give me a BREAK. That shit is so tired. Life's too short to play games! If you like a guy, just tell him! Whatever happened to love being about honesty and being

REAL? All those head games screw you up, confuse you, make life harder than it should be. Just listen to your heart, your gut.'

This philosophy troubles me deeply – because on some level I agree. Love *shouldn't* be about games. It should be a simple decision and action of the heart. It should be beautiful, evolved, unconditional and absolutely devoid of anger, guilt, resentment, hurt or betrayal. It should be a bond between two people who have magically managed to walk that fine line between being best friends and being lusty little Tasmanian devils in the four-poster.

But unfortunately, this would require all of us being on the same level of consciousness; all of us being aligned, sharing the same sentiments about being honest and upfront about how we feel, without fear of being hurt, or cheated on and left with nothing but the lounge and the blender.

Think about it. What good will it do if you're willing to love openly and with purity and honesty, but the men you're interested in are not at that same level of emotional intelligence? Of course, you'll move in circles filled with people who have a similar mindset to yourself, and it's possible to find a man who is on the same mental and emotional 'plane' as you. (If you find one, GRAB HIM!) But most of us are wandering around blindly through this big ol' world, and that's why we need to engage in the kind of 'games' detailed in this book: they act as a kind of screening process. An important reminder: it is essential, it is absolutely critical, that **you are capable of living happily, man or no man.** All of the approaches that I bang on about in this book are intended to come from a place of contentment and inner happiness, not desperation and manipulation.

You must believe that love can be unpolluted, honest and unconditional, but like anything beautiful, desirable and of worth, you need to put some effort in to achieve it.

Here's why.

Point one: We aren't in the '50s anymore
Here's one thing the 'Life's Too Short' school forget when they're spouting their little theories: love is a lot harder than it used to be. Nan and Pop were living in a very different time. Very. *They didn't even have rollerblades or Skype*! Fifty years ago people met, married and began breeding within a year, and all often before the age of 23. On the one hand this was a beautiful arrangement, because rather than over-thinking it – wondering about whether the grass might be just that little bit juicier over the fence, and had they made the right decision, and would Dane the Personal Trainer have been a better choice – couples just agreed they were in it for life and worked to make it work. However. Women didn't have one-eighteenth the awareness about who they were and what they were capable of. We were only just figuring out we could have a career too, and were not necessarily confined to the roles of wife and mother, for instance.

Fast-forward to the 21st century and we women are pretty complex beasts. We're not prepared for 'settle' for the high-school sweetheart or the first man who compliments us on our hair in the Big City. We know what's out there (thank you, intermernet) and we want

Hey hey hey, now! 'Secretary' as well. (Joking! I'm on your team)

to make sure we're making the right decision. Sometimes to the point of paralysis.

Point two: We can afford to say 'no' to a relationship now

These days, we have it all – independence, finances, career, sexual liberation, emotional awareness and the ability to write books about dating while juggling full-time work and growing popularity as a street mime.

With all of this comes the need for a little more from our relationships than a ring and a picket fence. Because while we don't *need* men anymore, we still very much *want* them. And there is a vast difference. Ultimately, we have a lot going on, we have a lot to offer – why should we waste time with a man who is unsuitable, or badly matched, or a cheater, or abusive or dull?

The majority of women now enter relationships with a certain degree of intellectual and emotional awareness. Having come this far, why should we just chuck all of our assets into a basket and offer it to the first guy who comes along who buys us a margarita or asks for our number?

Point three: Evolution is a *really* slow process

While we've evolved intellectually and emotionally, our fundamental physiology hasn't changed much. We are modern minds living in ancient bodies. Our bodies still issue a fight-or-flight response when we're pissed off with a driver who cuts us off in the traffic – but is that helpful to us? No. We're not about to be eaten by a Velociraptor, we're just about to lose our spot on the exit ramp.

There's less clubbing girls over the head these days, but the desire to win hasn't changed much since we lived in one-bedroom studio caves.

The simple fact is that, as it stands, men are still wired to gravitate towards the hunt. They enjoy the chase; they love a challenge. They value that which provides them an opportunity to be brave, powerful and all-conquering over that which requires them to make little or no effort.

And no matter how smart, impressive or influential we women are, that will not change. Do you honestly think you're the exception to a system that has been operating since before Jesus was given his first pair of sandals? I mean, you're pretty amazing, but you're not *that* amazing.

FIELD REPORT

Lil' Miss Life's Too Short is everywhere. She might be your sister. Or your best friend, or your happily married Aunty Lorna. Everyone comes at relationships from their own angle and with their unique life experience. But you must remember that *their angles are wrong* and mine is totally, 100% right. If life's too short, then life's too short to settle for an ass of a man.

This is not the same Eve that ate the apple. There's no way Zoë is old enough to know her.

One friend of mine, Eve, provides a perfect example of why life isn't too short to throw in all common sense. She met a guy at a friend's thirtieth. They clicked, they pashed and he got her number.

Three days pass, no call. He texts on Wednesday evening: *Hey Eve, great to meet you the other night. Are you free Friday night?* Eve responds in the affirmative, some banter ensues and the date is set.

They go and have a great time. Saturday and Sunday pass, again, no contact from him. Eve calls me.

She's starting to doubt herself. Maybe she was boring or not pretty enough. I tell her she's insane and to relax.

So she consults her flatmate, who tells Eve she has tampons for brains and should call HIM. Eve is now *very* confused. She knows she 'should' wait for him to contact her, but it feels unnatural, and anyway, how old is she? What era are we in? She can call him, surely? Waiting around is for chumps.

So she calls. He answers on the last ring with a hurried 'Hello.' He sounds busy. She stammers and says it's Eve. They chat for a few minutes but he seems distracted. Turns out he's about to play squash with Giles and Thomas. Eve hangs up the phone feeling like cow excrement. She wishes she hadn't called him – she doesn't like the feeling of being a nuisance, even though he was friendly enough on the phone. She vows not to call him again. She can do without this feeling – it's awful. She prefers the feeling of seeing his name show up on her phone instead. She decides to give him one more day to call, and then if not, he's in the Not Right bin. She refuses to start doubting herself because he can't be arsed to call her.

She gets on with life and he calls three days later. She misses the call, he leaves no voicemail message (no voicemail message doesn't count as a true call) and he texts her one week later. Eve decides that if it takes him a week to want to see her again, he's not only lazy, he's a fool. I tell her she is my Most Awesomest Friend ever and reward her with a new pair of Gucci shoes (or a noogy on the head – can't remember which).

In his defence, it could have been a really long squash game. Although, possibly more likely, he's going cold.

THE HARDCORE LOVE GUIDE THAT LOOKS PRETTY INSANE BUT IS REQUIRED IN THE VERY EARLY DAYS

EVENT	MAKE CONTACT?	WHICH KIND?	WHEN?	NOW WHAT?
You've just met him	Hell, no			He'll contact you. If he doesn't, forget about him ASAP.
He calls, you miss it	No, he'll call again. Wait.			*Wait*, I said. Gosh!
He contacts you asking to see you	Yes	Same medium as his	After at least an hour	Wait for his response
After a date	No, he'll contact you. You've said thank you at the end of the date already.			When he does text, respond about how much fun you had. Unless you had zero fun, in which case, delete and move on.
He texts to see if you're out on a Friday night	Well . . . *are* you out? (Trick question: it DOESN'T MATTER.) No response. Be strong.			Respond the next morning, happy you saved yourself from possibly ending up doing shots/ karaoke/ sexual acts with him.

He emails during the day	Yes	Email	A few hours after he emailed you. Remember: instant gratification takes your Perceived Value down.	Receive his response, write back in turn, let him respond again, then hold off. Always let his email be the last sent for the day.
He throws rocks at your window at 2 a.m.	Yes	Halved oranges, preferably frozen	Immediately	Duck
He wants a follow-up date the day after prior date	Yes, to tell him you're busy all week, save for Wednesday.	Text message	Hour or two after he contacts you.	See if he too is free Wednesday, otherwise say it will need to be next week.

HANDY HINT

Whenever you get the urge to call him, imagine him seeing your number coming up on his phone, frowning and then putting his phone back in his pocket. Oh sure, it's harsh. Real harsh. Harsher than a brand-new kitchen scourer on your cheeks. But if you insist on calling men when they should be calling you, you need some harsh.

Next time you're doubting your willpower, or a friend tells you to man up and call *him*, ask yourself this: if life truly is too short, then why should I spend it wondering if he really likes me? Why would you do that to yourself? And why do you have so much time to worry about one phone call, from one guy?

Not getting a call is way more impactful on a guy than any conversation you could have with him Even if it involves brilliantly witty, topical observations and reasons as to why Christopher is your favourite 'Sopranos' character.

WHAT HAVE YOU LEARNED?

The bottom line is that if a man has just met you, and was lucky enough to be dazzled by your wit and charm, but he's not calling to lock you down for coffees or movies or 'this great little pizza restaurant I know', then you don't call him to remind him of your existence. He knows you're there, he has your number, or at the very least your name and thus the ability to find you on Facebook, and he has chosen not to contact you.

No one's too busy to call. Even Obama found time to call Kevin Rudd, and you know that can't have been a priority.

Why are you wasting precious hours thinking about him when he thinks so little of you he can't even be arsed texting or calling you?

By **calling him**, you're reaching out to a guy you've barely met in the hope that he'll respond in accordance with your (now pretty high) expectations, by:

A. being available to talk at that time, and thus not having to brush you off à la Eve's story above, which makes you feel like shit since you're already full of nervous energy calling him in the first place;

B. appearing to be pleased to hear from you; and

C. feeling compelled to ask you out on your terms, or say yes if you're asking him out.

Not calling him indicates both strength and self-confidence. By carrying on with enjoying your life regardless of whether your phone vibrates and flashes with bright lights, you're showing that you value your time and your emotional energy, and that some guy you just met doesn't control your life according to whether he decides to bestow you with a phone call.

Now, you tell me: which is the more self-respecting option?

It can be an awkward mental leap to say to yourself, 'I play games', but that's because you're thinking it's like a murderer leaving clues for the police. But it's a lot less conniving than that. Think less about 'games' and more about an 'obstacle course' that any decent guy should be able to get through if they want you, while the duds are left panting and crying because they can't pull their fat arses over that big wall in the middle (you've seen army movies, you know the one).

11.

Engage the Apricot

In this lesson, you'll learn how to be more like a sweet, delightful stone fruit than a hard-edged marine mollusc.

While there are over three billion types of woman out there, each of us wondrous in our own way, there is a specific kind of woman men *particularly* love. Always have. She's the perfect blend of all that men are *supposed* to want (brains, self-confidence, motivation, independence) and everything men *really* want (softness, vulnerability, ability to nurture, just the right amount of dependence). And she has a pink convertible, a pink house and a boyfriend called Ken.*

*who has a blank spot where his genitals are, so you know you could come in and steal her off him

No, really. I promise you that it's entirely possible to be both. In fact, we all are, on some level. It's the Yin and the Yang, the feminine and masculine sides, working in harmony to create a woman who is both strong and soft. And when you're single and meeting men, it really helps to know how to balance the two. Whatever your disposition, though, it's crucial you have a powerful core of confidence and self-worth deep in your belly, anchoring your softness and your strength.

A lot of women I know and work with have the tough exterior. Maybe this is because we've spent so much time busting our guts on our career and being successful and independent, proving that we're tenacious and savvy enough to endure in a Man's World, that we haven't spent enough time nurturing our softer side. Or for some it may be a result of a nasty relationship, or a disgusting break-up, or even deeper, more serious events in our past that hinder us from showing our more vulnerable, softer side more often.

It's important to evaluate if your current balance of light and shade is working, or if you need to adjust it a little. Maybe you need to turn down the assertive dial and ramp up the gentle.

Really? you have two dials? we're all learning something in this book.

Consider these questions:
- Do you suck it up, repressing things that upset you because you never like to hurt people's feelings?
- Do you have a shiny, impenetrable veneer that people find intimidating?
- Do you let fly without a moment's notice and then regret it for days later?
- Are you constantly being bent over because you're too giving?

While there is a broad range of female characteristics, I believe a lot of us fit into either the apricot or the oyster archetype, exposing the qualities to greater/lesser degrees. For romance, I strongly advise the apricot over the oyster. Sure, there's less zinc and your apricots

Also, if you fall asleep in the sun, you definitely don't want to be the oyster.

won't go as well with that bottle of Veuve Clicquot, but trust me on this one.

The Oyster

Since our bra-burning foremothers began paving the way for us, a lot of women have been subtly encouraged to act like an oyster. This is where you maintain a tough, hard outer shell (or at the least the illusion of one), but you're soft inside. The slimy little pearl-producer survives in a very stressful environment but manages to retain an inner softness and beauty. The oyster can help in the boardroom. But when you're dealing with matters of the heart, the oyster is a terrible choice. In fact, behaviour to the exact contrary will be profoundly more beneficial.

The Apricot

Ah, apricot. Baby-cheek soft on the outside, but on the inside we find an industrial-strength stone, capable of breaking a human tooth – *maybe even a chainsaw*. What a style: maintaining a sweet and adorable exterior, and all the while nursing a core of solid, unbreakable resolve. How powerful this combination can be when you wish to expose your integrity and assertiveness with flair and mind-boggling finesse. You say what you need to, but frame it in sweetness and light so no one ever thinks anything of you other than that you're an utter delight.

worms also love you, but this just proves that no creature can resist your allure.

THE POWER OF THE APRICOT

My dear friend Audrey called me recently to ask me for advice. A guy she had been seeing wanted to take her out to a movie and dinner. The only thing was he was asking her, via text, at 4.58 p.m. on the day he wanted to take her out. I told her it was obvious from his actions that either his previous plans for tonight fell through, or he's so arrogant that he actually thinks you'll be free with three hours notice. It was time for her to Engage the Apricot, even though she VERY, VERY MUCH wanted to go on this date with him.

Here was her response: 'Hi Daniel, I'd love to go to dinner and a movie with you tonight – that sounds like so much fun – but unfortunately, I already have plans . . . Thank you all the same, though.'

See? Soft as a kitten's ear on the outside, hard as a PhD in astrophysics in the middle. Audrey was polite and gracious, but made her point clear. He didn't need to know she was annoyed with his shitty notice, all he had to know was that she was unavailable and perhaps next time he should call a little earlier in the week.

The apricot is about maintaining but concealing your strength. There's no need to show you're upset with guys who don't meet your expectations. Just sweetly inform them you're not going to indulge their sloppy behaviour and keep smiling. Now, you might be thinking that the whole 'sweetheart' part sounds revolting and evolutionarily retarded. But don't be fooled. This is about respecting yourself without making a song and dance about it.

The alternative – becoming angry or upset with a guy who isn't treating you properly – doesn't leave him thinking you deserve better treatment. He'll be quite glad he's not going on a date with you after all.

Instead, your firm but sweet-as-pie rebuff will make him sit up and take notice. He'll learn that he's done

I promise you, in Daniel's head he is panicking that the ship to Fun Island has sailed without him on board.

the wrong thing and you're left looking calm, in control and still desirable. It's also helpful when he *knows* he's been doing the wrong thing by you. He expects a cup full of crazy so when your response is clear but nonchalant, you baffle him – and then you can let him go, because you've got better shit to do. The surprise forces him into self-examination. This generally leads to a positive result: you've asserted your boundaries in the most graceful manner possible, and he recognises that you are a woman to be reckoned with.

TYPICAL REASONS WOMEN EMPLOY 'THE APRICOT'

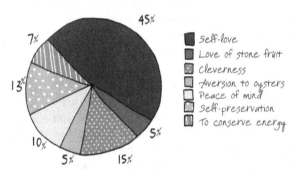

45%

7%

13%

10%

5%

5%

15%

5%

- Self-love
- Love of stone fruit
- Cleverness
- Aversion to oysters
- Peace of mind
- Self-preservation
- To conserve energy

The secret to driving us mental (and let's not beat around the bush, that's what this book is about) is to always make us feel like we just missed out on the best thing ever. If a guy jerks you around, don't send messages like an angry local council that is extremely upset with the state of its nature strip, send him a postcard from Fun Town (the capital of Fun Island, which we mentioned a page ago) to let him know he missed out. One form of correspondence ends up in the bin, one ends up on the fridge.

module two:
dating

1.

That Whole Sex Thing

In this lesson, you'll learn the appropriate time to engage in sexual relations with a man.* And then probably ignore it, guffaw and carry on a bit and do what you want to anyway.

Wu-*hey*! Look at you! You've flown with elegance and caution through the valley of courting and successfully parachuted down into the forest of dating. Or something. In any case, *well done*! You're dating! I should warn you here that things are about to get very interesting. And by 'interesting', I mean 'enjoyable, potentially thorny but always rewarding'.

Let's recap on where you're at:

- You have attracted a man who wants to see you again.
- Not only did you allow him to make the first move, you encouraged The Chase by being confident, and having an excellent, fulfilling life and not waiting around for a man to make you happy, and you've had a few kick-arse dates with him.

*My housemate just paid me $50 to say, 'Engage right now, even if you don't know his name!!!', but I won't cloud your judgement like that. Especially if you could pay me, say ... $60? Think about it.

- You like him but you know your worth, and some guy, as delightful as he might be, doesn't throw your world upside down just because he shows a little interest.

There comes a time in every single woman's life when she realises that perhaps she needs to buy some groceries, because wine, leftover Thai and a couple of condiments wasn't what she imagined the sum contents of her fridge would be at the age of 28.

But only if the bongos consent and there is a safe word.

There also comes a time when she meets a guy, starts dating him and needs to decide when she and he will bang the bedroom bongos. He *would* have more say in the decision, except that having sex on the bar the first time he meets her is (strangely) considered socially unacceptable . . . The topic (or act) of s-e-x is going to happen soon. Tonight even! (Have you waxed? *Don't*. You *never* get lucky if you've waxed.)

There are two ways to go about the whole sex thing. You can go for **casual sex**, which men have been doing for several millennia, and which implies you go in and leave with no expectations. (See also: booty calls, hook-ups, friends with benefits, no strings attached.)

Or you can go for **smart sex**, which is a little more complicated because it means you don't get instant gratification – and most people don't like that – and it infers you might like to enjoy a real-life relationship with this person.

Choosing which to go for will depend on your long-term plans with this particular man. So work it out: **is this going to be casual sex, or the start of a quality relationship?**

CASUAL SEX

It is probably going to be casual sex if:

- The thing that attracted you to him in the first place was his smooth moves at the bar, (even though you're clever enough to know men who use smooth moves on women never really stop using them, whether in a relationship or not).
- He's fun and it's all very light-hearted.
- He's an ex of a friend and you know it can't go anywhere 'serious'.
- You think about his rippling biceps more than his sparkling wit.
- You're genuinely interested in a 'low-investment-high-return' deal with this man.
- He lacks almost everything from your list (see Module One, Lesson 5).
- He's a playaaaa.
- He's ten years younger than you, and that's a deal-breaker for you.

  If you're 18 though, the illegality of it should be the deal-breaker.

- Either or both of you have just fallen out of a loooong relationship and know *exactly* what you need. And it's not celery.
- You don't find yourself waiting for him to contact you obsessively, because you know he will, and if he doesn't, well, meh.
- You have NO desire to have breakfast with him the Morning After and you watch the clock till it's 6 a.m., when you can kick him out because you 'have to get ready for work'. On a Sunday.

What this means
Well, to be honest, it means you can put this book

down for a while. You can stop it with The Chase. You can text him when you like, you can even – gasp – call *him!* I know, I know, someone has just bought a one-way ticket to crazy town and the name on the ticket is the same one as the one adorning the front of this book.

This is the difference between picking up a hot 22-year-old for sexy times, and meeting a 35-year-old who seems to be clever, funny and straight.* The difference between wanting to pinch his bum, and wanting to introduce him to Mum. If you're only interested in slaps and giggles, you can take a completely different approach to men and dating from those looking for a relationship.

*It's not just 13 years, although well done to those who spotted that.

But! This is dangerous territory for most women, because like it or not – and despite those who subscribe to the Samantha Jones School of Sexual Liberty – women are simply not equipped for emotion-free, string-free, love-free sex. We're not. Deal with it. Men, on the other hand, are. They were designed to spread their seed to as many as possible; we were meant to take the first seed,* uh, 'planted' in us and breed immediately.

*Sometimes referred to as 'SeedTron 5000™', or 'player', depending on whether or not the guy himself gets to name it.

You need to ensure you're not kidding yourself about your emotional strength, and your expectations, if you're going to engage in casual sex. Especially if you are newly single and think you're a lot stronger than you actually are inside. You say you definitely don't want to ramble down the road to a relationship with this guy, so are you happy to just hang out with him for one of these reasons?

1. You think it will be enjoyable to have sex with him.

2. You want to date men randomly (and sleep with them if you choose) for a while, because you can, and it'll make your married friends jealous.

3. He's a bit of fun, and you're a bit of fun, and that makes one full fun.

Yes? Well then, *great!* You are *almost* ready to light those candles, pour that glass of wine and put on the CD of that soulful guy whose name you can't remember but who's very sexy. But first? (Change from light-hearted jazzy music to ominous strings and organ), let's make sure you're REALLY ready (in your head – we know the rest of you is good to go).

TAKE A TEST

Answer yes or no to determine if you're *really* ready to knock boots with no expectations:

1. Do you know what he does for work?

2. Do you care?

3. Do you want him to meet Kate and Jess and Bec?

4. Do you fantasise more about being naked with him than being hand-holdy and sunset-watchy with him?

5. If you were to text him first (against the rules of The Chase) for a hook-up, and he didn't respond, or responded in an uninterested way hours later, would you be okay with that?

6. If you were to get drunk and text him for a hook-up (also against the rules of The Chase) and you didn't hear back till the next day, would you feel jealous or down?

7. When you wake up after a night with him, do you feel bad, used or like you've betrayed yourself in any way?

8. When he doesn't call you after a night with him, after you told him you didn't need him to because 'it's just hooking up', do you feel hurt?

9. When you see him with other girls on Facebook or out at a bar, do you feel a pang of rage or ouch?

10. When you meet a guy you genuinely want to start a Quality Relationship with, do you find it hard to switch out of hook-up mode?

If you answered, 'who cares? Rooting's awesome!', then you're clearly a guy who's stolen this book off a girl, and we kindly ask you to give it back. (Although that does provide an insight into the male attitude towards casual sex.)

The Correct Answers

1. No
2. No
3. No
4. Yes
5. Yes
6. No
7. No
8. No
9. No
10. No

If you answered any of these questions incorrectly, I suggest you spend a little more time thinking about the REAL reasons you want casual sex and whether you're genuinely equipped for it. A friend, Betty, told me she wanted to sleep with this guy she'd met a month back, and with whom who she'd been texting. She was annoyed that he kept *nearly* instigating a hook-up but then never following through. Also, she'd found she was texting him first and then getting no reply, or getting one that disappointed her. So, to get him out of her head she decided she'd make it happen, and in the process, show him she SO didn't want anything more than sex. Her plan was to look absolutely FUCKING amazing at a mutual friend's party, shag him with all she had, and then never call him again. I asked her if she would be okay with the idea that he wouldn't even care or notice that she never called him again, because it kind of looked like he might be that way inclined, and if so, what was the sting in her grand plan again exactly? Giving him hot sex with a hot girl? Ouch. Poor bastard. She realised then that she secretly hoped he would call her after the Amazing Sex, and admitted she would be gutted if he didn't . . . taking her back two steps when she was pretending it was going to take her five forward.

This type of punishment is up there with someone annoyingly sprinkling diamonds in your bed, or a Victoria's Secret model subjecting you to a rigorous tickling.

So! Be sure there aren't underlying negative reasons for your desire for casual sex:

Are you craving attention? Adoration? Ego-stroking?
Are you trying to prove something to yourself?
Are you trying to prove something to other people?
Are you on a revenge tirade from That Fucking Ex?
Are you trying to fill a Blank Space with empty sex?
Are you a serial killer with a highly sexual aggressive nature?

IMPORTANT

While string-free sex will appease your sexual appetite, it won't quench any deeply rooted needs for emotional fulfilment that might be lingering under all that lingerie. Ultimately, however fun they are,

They're the plastic fruit of the relationship world – they seem appetising (can even be impressively big), yet ultimately, not real.

hook-ups feed the body but starve the soul. They create a pattern of emotional detachment that can be *very* hard to break out of when something real shuffles into the spotlight, and they're rarely a positive thing for your self-esteem.

So, if you're gonna dive in, just be aware of what you're diving into, exactly. (Hint: It's not custard.)

Okay! Now over to the other side of the bed.

QUALITY RELATIONSHIP

It is probably the start of a quality relationship if:

- When you first met him, you had a minor, and mostly enjoyable, cardiac arrest.
- You have become a Phone Checker, even going so far as to take your mobile white-water rafting so as not to miss a call from him.
- You think of him as the potential Father of Your Children.
- You want eeeeeveryone to meet him and bring him up in conversation 78 times a day.
- You cannot Googlestalk him enough.
- You keep all your plans tentative in case he swoops in with one.
- You workshop every text from him – and those not from him but that you wish were from him – with friends.
- You DO NOT want to fuck this one up.
- You read books like this to make sure you don't fuck this one up.

Bad if he's in Witness Protection ... but then again, best you find out now.

Don't read my bits.

What this means

You probably don't want to shimmy into the sack too

soon. It's just like anything else at the embryonic stages of a relationship: you gotta test the waters before you dive in.

Why?

- Sex is an extension of your Perceived Value. If you're interested in a Quality Relationship, having sex on the first night *probably* doesn't throw a massively high Perceived Value out there. Remember: what comes too easily is generally considered to be of low value.

- Holding out (for at least a little while) is always beneficial. I'm not talking about ten weeks. (Despite my seductive mood lighting, we are not in the Dark Ages.) The fourth date is fairly standard, but if you can hold out till the sixth or seventh, magnificent. You will know when it's right.

- Don't forget or take for granted that feverish, hair-tugging making-out and frantic frottage is one of the most underrated activities in the world. There are few times in your life when you get to fool around messily with a guy without the expectation of sex. EMBRACE IT WHILE YOU CAN OR I WILL WRITE THE REST OF THIS BOOK IN CAPS LOCK.

Remember, you do need to eventually give in to The Chase. If either of you is worried about damaging a new hip during your 'first time', you may have left it too long.

Also, let us not beat around the proverbial. Sex is better when you've had to wait for it. Ask anyone who's ever had a secret crush on their partner's best friend – even the *idea* of sex you're not allowed to have is mind-bogglingly tempting. You see, mind and brains aside, our bodies have something to say about sex, too. When we have sex, we release the hormone dopamine, which is the one responsible for good times and lol-lipops and sunshine and laughter. Research shows that a reward acquired early, or before it was thought it would've been achieved, reduces the intensity and duration of dopamine activity in the brain . . . but a delayed reward *increases it*.

In non-science speak: The longer you make a man wait, the more excited and stoked he'll be about finally getting that 'reward'.

which increases the likelihood of post-coital cuddling, increases his respect for you, and therefore decreases the chances of bedroom flatulence. So it's Win-Win-Win for you, and Win-Win-clench for him

SEX AND THE CHASE

Don't delude yourself into believing sex is not an inte-gral element of The Chase. Oh, sure, there'll always be stories of couples who shagged on the first date and have been happily married for 600 years, but for every one of *those* tales, there are four billion stories of a girl sleeping with a guy because she thought, why not, I'm empowered and I can do as I please and if he judges me, well fuck him . . . and so she did, literally, and he faded out of her life soon after.

To break it down: if you hand over the keys to your lady garden too early, some men will pick their vegetables and rack off over the back fence before you've even had time to notice they were stealing your pumpkins.

It all goes back to a) men instinctively being drawn to The Chase; and b) you treating yourself with self-love and respect, and admitting that while you are rife with randy thoughts, denying yourself that instant gratification stands to win you so much more.

If you don't value yourself enough to show him that your naked body and those wild little moves you read about in *Cosmo* are worth waiting for, why would *he* value you?

HANDY HINT

The next day is always weird. Always. Whether you want to see him again or not. But like a spectacular hangover (and you may well have one of these, too, which never helps the Dark Thoughts), it will pass. Tomorrow, those wicked little flashbacks (the ones that cause you to cover your mouth, or close your eyes, or shake your head in order to avoid them exploding into your mind) will have calmed and your head will be screwed on straight again. Try not to watch your phone too much and keep yourself busy. Tomorrow you will feel 200% again.

Fact: Guys are always trying to make you sleep with them. Since not many of us have mastered hypnosis, we have had to resort to other, just as deceitful, tricks. Such as lying. Saying 'I really respect you for that', when you sleep with us on the first date, actually means the opposite.

WHAT HAVE YOU LEARNED?

The girl who gives it up after one text, one call, one bowl of risotto, half a bottle of wine and one night will not be thought of as being as desirable and self-valuing as the girl who only gives it up after 12 calls, 18 texts, six dates and five make-out sessions. She just won't. And you know it.

Hamish's final thought: The key here is finding a happy medium yes, there is no glory in conquering a castle with all its doors open and a trail of M&Ms leading inside, but if a guy feels he is ramming against the castle wall with no response, he'll eventually go find a castle with slightly easier walls to break down.

2.

Never Drink and Text (Ever)

In this lesson, you'll learn how to harness your inner mobile-phone strength and adopt some strategies about why, when, how and what to text.

One of the most frustrating elements of dating, aside from wondering if he has any of those unsavoury STIs you should know about, is wondering when you should text him, what you should text him and why you should text him back when he absolutely does not deserve it.

In this lesson you'll learn how best to handle the inevitable mindfuck that comes from having just met a guy you like, and whom you think likes you, and with whom you now enter the world of boundary-setting experiments and expectations that is mobile phones and their SMS function.

Obviously, no two men or women, or situations, are alike, but there are some general guidelines to follow in these early days. These rules exist not so you can torture him, or make him feel small and powerless, or make him think you're a super hardcore bitch who probably owns several Rottweilers and a fully equipped army tank with a penis-destroying missile projector. They're here so you can create a template for the rest of your time together.

Always begin your relationship in the manner in which you would like it to continue for its duration.

For example: when you've just started dating, if you allow him to think it's acceptable to tell you he'll text you later that day and then you don't hear from him for two days,* what on EARTH, WIND OR FIRE makes you think he'll suddenly change his habits midway through your seventh month together and start being more considerate? He won't! No chance! Forget it! Not on your life! Pass me those chips! And that dip!

You have to, *have to* be honest with yourself from the early days about what you're willing to accept and what you won't. If you have been following all of the lessons in this book, this should come naturally, because you'll be in a frame of mind I call 'positively selfish', and far more capable of sussing out the desirable men from the disingenuous. (Desirable: the guy who calls you on a Tuesday; disingenuous: the guy who calls on Friday.)

DATING DICTIONARY: POSITIVELY SELFISH

Maintaining a high and happy state of emotional wellbeing; enjoying a window of time (no matter how brief) of having no men consuming any mental real estate whatsoever; putting yourself first; revelling in coming home late and not having anyone to answer to; not checking your phone 256 times to see if he has

Or: why you shouldn't marry your boss if you're the nanny.

*Could be the extremely rare circumstance that all his fingers were broken and it took him two full days to write the message.

(Magical: the one who has already called next Friday.)

Though your penchant for breakfast foods at night, could be a turn on, especially for the lazier amongst us.

called or texted when you're out with your girlfriends; and eating porridge for dinner if you feel like it: these are elements of what it is to be 'positively selfish'.

Now. Don't think for a second that he won't be making the same assessment of you (though without the 'positively'), and rapidly. This is why lots of guys drop off after a little while when you're enabling The Chase and being a Clever Single Woman. They can tell right away that you're a lady who knows what she wants, and sometimes, as detailed in Module One, this can scare a guy off if he thinks he'll be incompatible with those needs, or isn't in the same headspace, or is simply after some casual sex.

This is okay. Perfectly okay. In fact, it's honourable for him to drop out of the race and hand it over to guys who are prepared to treat you well. And it's better to know from the outset that he's not the thoughtful, considerate type, rather than on your first wedding anniversary when he completely forgets and goes to the pub to watch the football and get shitfaced with the 'fellaz', right? *Right?* Fricken A.

If you make dating you the equivalent of the Olympic Marathon, then only the few and the brave will pursue. (Also handy if you really like Kenyans.)

YOU HAVE ONE NEW MESSAGE

Typical times we hope/expect he will contact us

- Within three days of meeting us
- After a date
- After making out with us
- After sleeping with us
- When he is overseas/away
- When he tells us he will
- When he texts, and we text back and it's his turn
- When we text him

- On the day of a date to confirm said date
- On the day of your wedding to confirm said date

Typical times he doesn't contact us and we lose the fucking plot
- Within three days of meeting us
- After a date
- After making out with us
- After sleeping with us
- When he is overseas/away
- When he tells us he will
- When he texts, and we text back and it's his turn
- When we text him
- On the day of a date to confirm said date
- On the day of your wedding to confirm said date

How does this happen? Mismatched expectations. Expectations are founded on the premise that other people, things or situations will behave in a way that is in accordance with how you think they should. But as we all know, they rarely do. *Especially* when it comes to men and their mobile phones.

Take a girlfriend of mine – let's call her Margery – who was being dragged through an emotional food processor by This Guy recently. She was losing her shit because on Thursday he had proposed a huge list of fun and exciting activity for them for the coming weekend and then she didn't hear from him until the following Tuesday. She was ropable. Couldn't believe he could do this to her. What a prick. He needs a swift kick in the lap walnuts, and so on.

Her expectations were high because he had told her they should be, and so she was violently disappointed

Unless he had a really good reason, like he was going extremely well on a video game. Am I right girls? Am I? Are those crickets I can hear? That's weird, especially in print . . .

when they weren't met. *However*. The truth of the matter is that she is the only one who could assign importance to his actions. It was up to her how much she let it get to her. She could react wildly or calmly and confidently. When you have a solid core of self-confidence and self-respect, then if a guy does something that hurts you or lets you down, you don't lose your grip and start throwing shoes at walls in a feverish rage. You're calm and you don't take it personally. You understand that what he does can only affect you if you allow it to. You can choose to hold your head high, say, 'Whatevs, Trevs' and let him know he's blown it.

And it's a double blow, because statistically his name probably isn't Trevor, so you get to make him jealous too.

If Margery had known this, then perhaps when she hadn't heard from This Guy by noon Saturday, she would've told herself his time was up – his loss – and proceeded to make plans with friends, family or other dudes who think she is awesome. She would see pretty much straight away that wasting a whole weekend over a guy who couldn't even be bothered to contact her to follow through on his hyped promises was an EPIC FAIL on his behalf. And seeing as there are only 52 weekends in a year, he sure as hell wasn't going to ruin 1/52nd of them.

This flips it, by the way. We'll immediately panic and think you don't care, because you have someone better. Sneaky, and therefore – well done.

HOLD THE PHONE

Now, it's all well and good to say you're strong and emotionally mature enough to not get upset when he doesn't contact you although you really, really heartbreakingly hoped he would. I know, I really do. But it still hurts, and no book, not even one this rad, can tell you otherwise.

I have absolutely, one zillion per cent been there – frustrated, maddened, pissed off – and if you think I always manage to follow my own advice in these situations, you're a fool. (No offence.) We always teach that which we need to learn the most, as they say.

However, I know when I need to harden up. I know when it counts. I know not to sit around waiting for him to contact me, and I know not to desperately chase after him with messages too. I know to never SMS him when I am feeling like a frustrated T-Rex after 14 cans of Red Bull. I know that building up my Infrequent Caller Miles is crucial. I know how to send him a message by not sending him a message. And as a rule, it's when you want to contact him the most that you *must not*, because you're letting yourself down if you do. **You need to be stronger than ever when you are hurting the most.**

If you're having trouble not checking your phone constantly to see if he's been in touch, it's helpful to remember that it's preferable to make life a bit trickier for guys at this stage of a potential Quality Relationship than to be one of those women who immediately write back 'luv 2! xx' when a guy messages them on a Friday at 7.32 PEE EM asking if they would like to 'hang out' tonight. Just quietly, these women are fucking it up for the rest of us, who actually think that's one fat lame-arse attempt at a 'date' and he deserves a nuclear wedgie not a 'yes, please'.

Other things it pays to remember when you find yourself taking out your phone's battery to make sure there is nothing wrong with it, or calling yourself from your work phone to check the network isn't down:

Remember, we will always try the easiest option first; we're always looking for an unlocked door. But surely you're good enough to at least make him try the window, or attempt to parachute onto your roof.

- Obsessively checking your phone, email and Facebook is now viewed as being as much of an addiction as drugs, cigarettes or alcohol. Recognise that what you are doing is terribly unhealthy, *put the Goddamn phone down*, and for heaven's sake, go to the casino or have a hit of meth instead.

well, we might check it occasionally, but mostly it's for amusing video forwards. Sorry.

- He's not checking *his* phone to see if *you* contact him. He's not. The more you get this into your head, the easier not checking yours becomes.
- Your network has not suddenly 'dropped out', your battery is fine, *he just isn't calling you.*
- Don't you have stuff to do? Does your whole life go on hold while you're waiting to hear from him? Shit no! Call your mum! Read a book! Meet up with a girlfriend and eat pudding! Take a figure skating class! Take a pudding skating class!

HANDY HINT

If you simply CANNOT stop checking your phone, do what I do: put it on silent, ram it down into the bottom of your undies drawer, padlock the drawer shut and then place the key into a glass of water and freeze it. Handy, effective and only showing *mild* signs of mental dysfunction.

KRYPTONITE FOR YOUR SMS BAN

1. You're lonely on a Sunday afternoon.
2. You're feeling agitated by his lack of texting and decide you can 'fix things' by reminding

him you exist, with a text. (Hint: he knows you exist. He doesn't need a reminder.)

3. You see your ex with a new girl and want to 'get him back'.
4. You hear from a friend that she saw him out having a GREAT time last night.
5. You've been listening to a Life's Too Short person (See Module One, Lesson 10).
6. You're very hung-over.
7. You're very toey.
8. You're very lonely, hung-over and toey.
9. You're very drunk.

Let's go to a graph for a clear explanation for that last one.

HOW GOOD AN IDEA IT IS TO TEXT HIM WHEN DRUNK

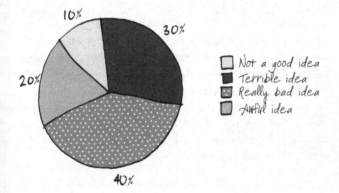

□ Not a good idea
■ Terrible idea
▨ Really bad idea
▤ Awful idea

WHAT HAVE YOU LEARNED?

What a man does may briefly enrage you, but you choose whether to let it eat away at you for days or move on. If he can't make the effort to contact you in these early stages of dating – this very short window of time in which to impress you – then surely you can see that you deserve better? If you can't, maybe come back and read this book once he's stomped on your heart a little bit and then we'll talk. Sorry, but sometimes we don't learn our lessons until we go through a particularly cruel brand of growing pain.

If you can stay strong and not contact him, even when it's BURNING you inside, you're scoring so many points for yourself and self-respect that if you were an NBA team, you would win the premiership for, like, ten years in a row. At least.

A guy fears nothing more than letting a good thing get away. If we're fishing and we think we feel a nibble, we're consumed with a primal desire to CATCH THAT FISH, BECAUSE IT'S PROBABLY AN AMAZING FISH THAT OUR MATES WILL WHISTLE ABOUT IN AN IMPRESSED MANNER. Then when we feel nothing on the line, the size of this hypothetical fish only increases, until we're convinced we let Moby Dick swim away. We're less impressed if a fish jumps into the boat and starts stuffing itself with garlic, lemon and chilli. I mean, don't get me wrong, a self-stuffing fish is an evolutionary miracle, but we still prefer the first mysterious one.

3.

Sweet Nothings Mean Just That: Nothing

In this lesson, you'll learn how to tell whether what he says ('I'll pick you up at eight, babe') is more important than what he does (arrives at 9.30, reeking of Scotch).

If he comes at 8.15 reeking of Scotch Finger biscuits, it's a line ball.

Ever had a guy whisper sweet nothings about all the things he wants to do with you, and how special you are, and how lucky he is to have found you, and you can actually hear your heart start to fill with small, animated pink love hearts...? And then by the Wednesday of the following week he's failed to make any real effort to see you, or take you to that movie he thought you two *had* to see, or even give you so much as a good solid text rally?

Yes. Me too. Not *real* fun, is it?

There are many, many more examples of this kind of words–action disconnect. They extend right through from the courting stages ('I'd love you to meet my parents . . .'), to marriage ('Honey, shoosh, I'll fix the shower this weekend'), and from women to men ('Of *course* I don't mind if you go out with the boys!').

I call these 'short-term morale-boosting lies'.

The Walk–Talk Theorem

If he walks the talk = excellent

If he only talks the talk = suss

If he doesn't talk *or* walk = probably a mannequin

The key is to not get lost in what your new beau says, but rather what he *does*. Visualise it like kitchen scales. Weigh his words on one hand and his actions on the other. Do they hold level or do the scales tip?

You must make sure your scales are even too. There's no point getting all self-righteous about all of this and then being a walloping great hypocrite. (Common errors here include: saying you don't care about him going out all night and then going apeshit when he staggers in at 6 a.m.; saying you love his friends but making it obvious you want to stab them in the eyes with forks; and saying you are a Pay Your Way girl, then sulking when you end up paying for dinner.)

Here's something you may not want to hear, but it's better this than more sweet nothings: men know how much we love the way their words make us feel. They know how much value we place on talk every single day of our lives, and that next to tapestry and baking, it's one of our favourite activities. But sometimes – and this must be true because a Real Life man told me it was – men know what women want to hear so they tell us exactly that in order for them to get what they want.

Oh come now, as if that's a surprise. As if you've never been guilty of the same thing. ('I'll be your best friend' or 'I'll do the dishes every night for a year'. Ring any bells?)

Fact: Apart from pet rocks, which do exactly what they promise, men are the most literal species on earth. If you say it, we will take it as gospel.

Thank you, Mel Gibson, for nailing that film ↗

ACTIONS SPEAK LOUDER THAN . . .

The fact that massively wise people and cultures the world over say the same thing shows how timeless and true it is that actions speak louder than words. (And the fact that many famous humans said it too shows they probably all had some prick of a friend who kept borrowing money and never paying them back.)

- *Well done is better than well said.* (Benjamin Franklin)
- *When deeds speak, words are nothing.* (African Proverb)
- *After all is said and done, a lot more will have been said than done.* (Author unknown) (Fool! Come forward and claim this brilliance at once!)
- *Talk doesn't cook rice.* (Chinese proverb) (My addition: Or stir-fry vegetables.)
- *As I grow older I pay less attention to what men say. I just watch what they do.* (Andrew Carnegie)
- *People may doubt what you say, but they will believe what you do.* (Lewis Cass)
- *Between saying and doing many a pair of shoes is worn out.* (Italian proverb)

Okay, okay, you got me, but keep it down.

SPOT THE INCONSISTENCY

His words: 'I don't care what my mates think. I don't care if they see how into you I am.'

His actions: Carries on like a macho pork chop when in the company of his mates, leaving you to wonder who came and extracted all of his loveliness before he arrived at the pub.

The inconsistency: Says something to calm your mind

and make you feel special when it's just the two of you, but does not back it up when the situation arises.

I believe in England they call this 'lying'. we have the same word for it here too, as we borrow a lot of their language.

His words: 'I want to be with you. She means nothing to me – I don't even see her anymore!'
His actions: Still calls this 'old friend', still hangs out with her, still Facebooks her.
The inconsistency: He's attempting to reassure you by telling you he's 'clean', while simultaneously doing exactly the same thing as he was before.

His words: 'I just want to see you every day! I'm falling head over heels for you . . .'
His actions: Doesn't call or text for three days after making this claim.
The inconsistency: If a guy tells you he wants to see you every day but then can actually wait every four or five days, *he doesn't want to see you every day.*

His words: 'You're the most beautiful woman I've ever been with.'
His actions: He used to date Halle Berry.
The inconsistency: Clearly a liar.

It should be said that it's not always calculated. A lot of the time, men *genuinely* want to reassure you and make you happy, and they have good intentions. Sometimes they say these things in the *hope* they will actually follow through with their actions, but then don't have the willpower or fundamental desire to do so. But the bottom line, in fact the one under the bottom line, is that words hold absolutely no value – NONE – until they are backed up with actions. (I am aware that this is a book, and hence *all* words, so to back up what I am saying I'll perform the entire thing as interpretive dance on YouTube so you know I mean it.)

IT'S UP TO YOU

In the end, it's not really *him* who is letting you down by not following through on his words. If you accept it, *you're* the one letting yourself down, because *you're* the one taking his words, not his actions, as the true indication of his intention. You're the one rationalising why he made a scene at the party that night, or why he caught up with that girl when he said he wouldn't, or why, when he promises you his loser of a brother 'Yak' won't be tagging along on your date, he always ends up coming. You're settling for the sweet nothings and in the end you get just that: sweet nothing.

> **HANDY HINT**
>
> Without knowing it, we give clues about who we really are every single day. This realisation is helpful if you're beginning to doubt the validity and honesty of his words, because you can start to pay attention to how he conducts himself, say, with his friends, or family or in business. Is he a hard worker who has lots of happy work-mates or clients, or does he have no qualms selling senior citizens faulty life insurance? Does he have good relationships with his family, or is he feuding with his brother and disrespectful to his mother? Does he owe people money? Does

If you start accepting words as currency, guys will expect it every time and never go back. Like if your local coffee shop started accepting a handful of dirt as an alternative way to pay for your latte, why would you switch back to money? (Apart from keeping your hands cleaner.)

he have a good circle of friends, or do they look like extras in a telemovie on gang warfare? These things will show you who he really is. You might think you're an exception, because he tells you he really cares for you, but you're not paying attention: **his words don't mean shit.**

Turn down his volume and watch his behaviour instead. And if the dots aren't connecting? Listen to your gut. If it's telling you something is amiss, it almost always is.

These are guys who are used to duping people. They're the carnies of the dating world. Face facts, you're never going to win that stuffed gorilla.

THE MASSIVELY IMPORTANT EXCEPTION

Sometimes – and try not to get confused here – *sometimes* what he says is FAR more important than what he does. Let me explain.

If you hear him say anything along the lines of the following, get your sneaks on and walk very briskly to the door (I don't care if it's 12.03 a.m. and you're nude. You can grab a tea towel from the kitchen on the way out if you insist on being all prudish):

- You're too good for me.
- I'm not good enough for you.
- The next guy who gets you will be such a lucky man.
- You deserve to be happy.
- I just don't think I'm ready for a relationship.
- I'm off to backpack around Europe next month – *so* fricken pumped.
- I love the way we're both just so casual about this, and neither of us want a relationship or anything.

- Aren't fuck buddies the GREATEST invention EVER?
- You should *totally* meet my boyfriend, Michael.
- You know, my wife would love to meet you one day.
- So you *really* won't wear a nappy, huh?

These are his way of blatantly telling you he is **No Good For You** and you should disengage at once. ←

Ouch, yes. But if you think about it, it can *kind of* be viewed as admirable. Ultimately, if a guy tells you you're too good for him, or if he's already hinting at your next boyfriend, he's *probably* not going to be an excellent and loving partner, is he? If a guy thought you were the shit, he would be talking himself up and trying to convince you he was the best possible man for you.

you may as well, because in his head he's already gone, and in the European example, already fantasising about Swedish girls.

WHAT HAVE YOU LEARNED?

It's very easy to say 'I exercise every day', but to only run once a week. Or to say, 'I'd *love* to catch up and have lunch with you', and never follow up. You can say whatever you like if you want someone to believe something about you. Easy as. But when it comes to actually demonstrating something about yourself, it often becomes a lot more difficult.

You must learn the art of **ONLY valuing actions, NOT words**.

A girl I know, Corralie, thought she had found the world's dreamiest guy. She couldn't believe her luck – here was a genuinely decent man who seemed to say all the right things at just the right times. He was affectionate, adoring, romantic and *just* about to embark on an amazing new business idea. He was going to move out of his mum's place and buy a new car. Corralie couldn't believe this guy was still single. So motivated! So delightful! So good with a wok! And then a year passed. Still living with mum. Still driving the shitbox with no stereo. Still working at his mate's smash repair shop. Corralie started to see her dreams of marrying this man fade. Not only did it appear to be that his big-scale promises were bullshit, but he couldn't even manage to honour the little ones, like, 'I'm not going out this weekend', or, 'Of course I'll put some petrol in your car'. So she gave him an ultimatum, and he promised he would fulfil his end of the bargain. He did no such thing. She dumped him. We all cheered. (Except him.)

How many times has a boss promised you the world when you signed on for the job and then failed to come through with any of it? How many times have you felt let down when a girlfriend *promises* to return your dress/cash/Ferrari and then doesn't follow through, and the friendship disintegrates. How many times have you found yourself hurt or angry because a guy's words have not been backed up with action?

Pay attention when a man tells you he's going to do something. It might be that he *promises* he won't be late to pick you up anymore. Or that he's going to start staying at *your* place more often, because it's unfair that you always stay over at his. Or that he's going to cook you his special prawn lasagne. Or that he's sorry he took too much cocaine and acted like a douchebag, and he won't ever do drugs again.

Then watch. Just *watch*. Wait for the next time that

particular situation arises and see if he's modified his behaviour, as per his words. If there is any kind of disconnect between what he has said and what he is doing, you need to ask yourself if you can be with someone who can't make even the smallest improvements to his actions after promising he will – *especially in the early dating stages*. If he can't back up his words when he's trying to impress you, do you think he will suddenly begin to when he has 'secured' you?

There are real guys and then there are guys who have learned what to say to make them look like real guys. Do you want the guy who bellows, 'I'll save you!' when he sees you tied to the train tracks and then snatches you out of the way moments before a train rockets past (I've tried to pick an everyday example here, just to make it clear), or the guy that yells, 'I'll save you!' then adds, 'Straight after I've called Dave back'?

Remember, actions always beat words . . . But words beat rock, which beats scissors, which beats paper, which beats rock . . . hang on, that means paper might beat words too. Which just proves they're shit.

4.

The Thai and Tracksuit Pants Curse

you'll also learn that this was once considered as the title of the fourth Harry Potter book.

In this lesson, you'll learn that effort, courtesy, a healthy respect for romance and the ability to be able to sense what makes your partner happy are the keystones for a tremendous relationship. If these things are not evident from the formative stages, they never will be, and you'll have to suck it up because it's kind of your own fault.

It's time to pop on your silk scarf and your crystal pendants and take a look into the future.

It's important to understand that if a man isn't putting in much effort to begin with, he's not suddenly going to change and become the Super Attentive Romance-atron in six months, or six years, time. The amount of effort put in during the dating period is indicative of what it will be like in the future of the relationship. (Except that, uh, in most cases, after the dating period, it will likely be halved. So if there's bugger-all effort being put in at the beginning, there'll be half of bugger-all down the track.)

Like a job interview, except he'll steal fewer office supplies from you six months in.

FIELD REPORT

My friend Ruby met a Cool Guy out one night at a bar and he asked for her number. There were calls and texts and they had a coffee later that week. She gushed over their date and I could tell she liked him. A few days later he took her to dinner at a tapas bar and then a movie. The third date was a concert – they had a rollicking good time and made out at his place afterwards. Ruby told me that she 'kinda, maybe, liked him a little bit'. The following week there was lunch with him near her work; a few days later it was a dinner date at a tasty little Italian restaurant, followed by a few drinks and then back to his place to do some sheet tangling. Then a Friday night spent drinking and dancing followed by a sleepover at her place. For their next date, he suggested that they get some Thai and watch a DVD at his place. She thought this was a great idea. She didn't bother to do her makeup and arrived to find him wearing tracksuit pants. How cosy, she thought. What brand of loser would want to be out partying and single when you can be this comfy and relaxed?! A few days later, the happy couple got takeaway Japanese around for dinner, and on Friday night, it was pizza and a DVD, which he asked her to grab on her way over.

Can you see what has happened here?
If you said, 'The exploration of several international cuisines', you're correct, but missing the point. What happened is that within just a couple of weeks, the courting part (or 'hard' part) of this relationship (e.g., restaurants, picking up the girl, getting dressed up,

The guy is rapt. He's hung up both his collared shirts and knows he might not even need pants next time.

him choosing the movie and showing off his knowledge of cuisines, her bothering to blow-dry her hair) had already expired, and things had quickly segued into the comfortable (or 'easy') part (home dates, takeaway food and low expectations).

WHAT'S THE BIG DEAL?

I always cringe when a girlfriend tells me she spent the night on the sofa eating pizza with her new dude, especially if it's within a fortnight of having met him. She's not only failing to control the pace of the relationship (and if she is, she needs to get her brakes seen to, because it would appear they're faulty), but she has, in one pizza-crumbed moment, signalled that the Dating Phase has concluded and he can commence Phase 2, otherwise known as the Phase Where Things Start To Become More Familiar and Less Romantic.

you know that kid who goes all floppy at the supermarket and his mum has to drag him until he walks properly because he's tired and wants to lie down? He grew up. you might be dating him

Sadly, once you hit Takeaway-and-Tracksuit territory, you can pretty much kiss Proper Dates goodbye. (I told Ruby this, of course, but she had plenty of excuses as to why it was fine.)

'But that's *insane!*' you holler, probably standing next to Ruby. 'I can't have a casual Thai/DVD night if we're hung-over and it's Sunday night? What if he's a uni student? Are we supposed to get dressed up and go to a fucking five-star restaurant?'

No. You are not. (And I'd appreciate if you didn't swear unnecessarily, thank you.) But you *can* say to him, 'You know, I would *love* to see you tonight,' [*Engage the apricot!*] 'but I already promised my flatmate I would watch *Mad Men* with her . . .'

And even though you would like nothing more than

to fool around on the sofa with him, boasting bellies full of Pad Thai and green tea ice-cream, by holding off on the Cosy Stage you'll be doing great, great things for your relationship.

'But hang on,' you say. 'You're making assumptions here about what women classify as a date. What if I'm not a 'date' girl; what if I'm happy with take-away and television? We don't *all* need to gussy up and make our men spend on us, you know. Some of us are happy with the simple things in life – good company, nice food, clothing that is neither restrictive or breast-enhancing.'

To which I say, *good for you*. Truth be told, most of us fall into the category – and if we don't initially, we will do within a few weeks. Ruby's story is not an uncommon one. But here is the thing you might want to consider when you go around labelling yourself low-key and low-maintenance:

You cannot expect a man to suddenly whip out the dinner suit and book an incredible restaurant when you get that big promotion, if you've shown him in the past that such things are not important to you.

Also:

You cannot expect a man to know that this is simply 'the done thing', because part of his attraction to you was that you appeared not to care for these things.

Also:

When it's your birthday, and he makes little to no effort to show you a fabulous, romantic evening (be it in a park or the Park Hyatt), he won't understand when you lose your shit at him. At all.

If he wins you over using very simple, very low-effort dates, *what on earth* would possess him to think

Although there is a part of a guy's brain that says, 'This feels too easy ... something must be wrong'. Like the old pie-resting-in-the-middle-of-a-big-net trick.

that all of a sudden he's expected to start delivering tricky, thoughtful, high-effort dates? What part of you believes that he's nursing a core of extreme romance underneath those tracksuit pants? What makes you think he's the type to remember anniversaries, or leave little notes under your windscreen wipers, or buy a bottle of champagne to share on the day he buys his first unit?

It's like being hired for a job and being told that shorts, trainers and T-shirts are fine, and then your boss goes *sick* at you on the day of a presentation because you didn't know you were supposed to wear a slinky dress, heels and full makeup.

HOW TO AVOID THE THAI AND TRACKSUIT PANTS CURSE

1. Initially, allow him to choose the type of date and its venue – this will indicate how he thinks when it comes to romancing a *laydeh*.
2. This is not about expecting five-star fine-dining each time (an adorable little Chinese restaurant can be as romantic as Tetsuya's) – it's about the effort and thought put in.
3. Hold off on Thai and tracksuit pants for as loooong as possible. It'll make it all the more enjoyable when you finally succumb.
4. Put in some effort: show him that you take pride in your appearance and that you enjoy being able to dress up. If he feels proud of his sexy girl, why would he want to keep in her in fleece and watching a Nicolas Cage movie?

5. Encourage each other to try new cuisines – this will keep the dining game going longer. Treat each other to your favourite little places to eat – be it for breakfast, lunch, dinner or sacrificial suppers involving cloaks, caves and poisonous punch.

6. When he suggests some form of Thai and tracksuit pants evening, decline ever so politely. If he offers to cook for you, that's different. By all means let him and still dress as if it were a regular date. I remember my mum wearing her best dresses and perfume for home-cooked dinners that she'd decided were 'special' because of the time spent on them, or the invitation of a guest. This was partly because she never got a chance to wear them anymore, and partly because, well, *why not*? Why should the fact that you are at home mean you have to dress like a slob?

7. If there is anything you can celebrate together (he got a new laptop, you got a tax return), then celebrate. Even if it's beer and sandwiches on your balcony (cut up and served on nice plates of course). This subtly sets up a standard of quiet, adorable celebrating for years to come.

8. Stamp your foot and refuse to go if he offers anything less than a perfectly on-time pickup in a gold-plated limousine, a two-hats restaurant and a bunch of rare Persian roses. Ha ha! KIDDING! There's no such thing as a Persian rose. Obviously, he'd buy Bulgarian instead.

As long as this doesn't turn into Highmaintenanceville (last turn-off before Difficultistan), he'll make an effort. If it's done right, you're showing us the mould of the relationship you want, and all that's left for us to do is pour in our magic liquid relationship clay. Then bake for a few months. Then crack it out. Then paint it. The rest is up to you, I can't hold your hand forever.

WHAT HAVE YOU LEARNED?

Humans are pretty simple. We tend to rely on the fact that the manner in which things begin is the way they will continue to operate. By and large, established patterns or habits (in work, relationships, holidays) stick. Simple.

Ever heard yourself whine a few years into a relationship about how 'he's not like he used to be', or when a friend hooks up with a New Guy that 'she's changed so much', or when a new boss comes into the fold that 'she doesn't understand the way things work around here'?

You've noticed a change in the pattern, but you're still married to the old way, the original way of things, and this makes you feel somewhat confused and uncomfortable. So imagine Your Man watching as you throw a shoe at him because he forgot it was your birthday and you thought he was going to surprise you with dinner, or at least some fucking FLOWERS. He's there thinking: 'Who the hell *is* this woman? I don't recall her ever caring about any of this stuff! She told me flowers were transparent and that she'd prefer a BBQ over a fancy-shmancy restaurant any day, and *Jesus*, that shoe hurt.'

This is potentially fatal if she's a mountain climber and wearing those spiky boots.

If you're happy with casual dates, DVDs and take-away, and you HONESTLY won't be disgruntled when this is all you'll be enjoying in this relationship, then go ahead and order the Gai Yang. (I hear it's *amazing*.)

But if, like many women, there is a side of you that loves a bit of chivalry, a bit of romance, some thoughtfulness, a man who wants to make as much effort for you as you do for him, then you need to assert this at the very beginning. Because you can't teach old dogs new tricks and you can't teach old boyfriends new tricks either, which is probably more relevant. Trust me: if you two tumble into love, you'll have *years* of Thai and tracksuit pants, but usually less than six weeks of dating and dining. Soak them up.

Like a prawn cracker in Kung Pao sauce! ←

The trick to understanding guys is: We were happy in the womb and, apart from satisfying a few urges, we keep on trying to get back to that relaxed state. That is not good news for you, because a guy in the foetal position just gurgling lightly is not the ideal partner. But if you make yourself clear about how you want to be treated early on, then you will know: if we make an effort, we really do care.

5.

Beware the Self-Startler

In this lesson, you'll learn how to recognise – and avoid – the silky clutches of that most confusing and confused man, the Self-Startler.

Close your eyes for a moment and imagine a man who is very physically attractive (be specific – does he have a handlebar moustache? Abdominals of plutonium? A vast network of seafaring tattoos? Long, blond hair?) and incredibly attracted to you. Not only does he move in on you, with intense eye contact, and demand your phone number, he then proceeds to elegantly pursue you in the manner of most Hollywood films starring George Clooney. His texts are clever and sexy. His dates are interesting and new. His desire for you seems to be as unquenchable as bleached, dry hair that refuses to respond to anti-frizz treatment. You're so unaccustomed to being pursued in such a fantastical way that his attention almost embarrasses you. It almost seems too good to be true.

DINGDINGDINGDINGDING!

Hear that? No, of course, you're right – books

If this is your guy, the police would like to speak with him in regards to several crimes committed last April.

don't make sounds. (Except for the soft swoosh of your rapidly turning pages). But did you read that bold sentence of upper case 'dings' that implied some kind of warning bell? That's a warning bell. Because the man who does these things is generally going to end up being a Self-Startler.

Or audio books, by definition.

DATING DICTIONARY: SELF-STARTLER

A Self-Startler is a new suitor who comes on so strong, so fast, they scare themselves off.

He's the guy (or girl – we're absolutely guilty of self-startling too) who says the Right Things, does the Right Things, is affectionate and persistent and romantic, and whose behaviour indicates that if you were to *not* be near him, his ability to breathe may abandon him. He bowls in at 400 km/h, only to slam on the brakes equally as hard a few weeks – or sometimes even months – later.

So you can also pick him as the guy in the metaphorical neck brace.

Entirely fictional research indicates that the exact moment he decides to abort corresponds precisely to the moment you decide to finally 'give this thing a go'. Yes, the second that you decide to take him seriously and give in to all of his persistence, he realises, much to your incredulity, that despite propelling your romance at hurricane speed early on it's actually all going a little too fast for him, and he needs some space (or a hasty departure to Rio). And so he vanishes. Gone! Fades away! Along with his eight-SMSes-a-day habit, his bad poetry and his adorable quality of buying you a coffee on your way to work.

He may also play Spanish guitar to you. This is a self-startler favourite.

If you've never known the feeling of having your

mind boggled, this man will generously educate you. It is truly the most confusing thing to be cooed and wooed with such devastating passion and then to be abandoned cold, without so much as an exit interview. It's quite soul-destroying. And *that* is precisely why you need to be alert to the Self-Startler: to avoid a brand of unsavoury psychological damage that can linger and taint many a future relationship. *Gross.*

Thankfully, funk and jazz avoided destruction.

Treating a Self-Startler as you do any other guy doesn't have the same effect. What this means is that The Chase, holding off on calling him – in fact, all of your 'screening devices' – fall flat in the smiling, sucrose-dripping face of a Self-Startler. He doesn't care if you don't call. He'll call you. Twice. And then SMS you. And then pop into your office to see if you want to get lunch. Your steely resistance doesn't bother him. It enthuses and delights him. Your usual suss-out strategies before a relationship develops, which you use to see if he is going to be enjoyable or torturous, become null and void, because he is so keen to secure all of your headspace that he acts like a man who means it and yet does not actually mean it at all.

He has become adept at nailing an audition for a play he doesn't actually want to be in. He just wants to know he could get the part.

I know, I know, confusing. But this is why we need to rely on our heads and our guts, and not our hearts, in the early dating stages. Heart wants to get swept away with it all; head and gut ally to create a massive dam. Just as with anything in life, if your gut is telling you his behaviour seems disingenuous, it most likely is.

FIELD REPORT

A friend of mine, Mavis, was blown away by a classic Self-Startler recently. I could tell immediately what was happening – his constant references to the things the two of them would be doing in the future, coupled with his unattractive, competitive persistence to win her over, gave him away to me – but it's very difficult to warn a friend that the man who is throwing himself at her could be a love fraud. So, I kept it to a gentle, 'Honey, careful of this one. He could be more in love with the idea of love, than love itself', and let it be. Cut to two months later and he vanishes. Of course, this was just after her confession to me that she had put him through enough of The Chase and he'd proven himself.

He told her he was off to a music festival in another state and would be back Tuesday. Didn't call. Didn't come back Tuesday. She called him Wednesday. He'd decided to stay on, he said. Needed to clear his head. After a week of skeletal contact and my friend feeling like someone had just shut off her heroin supply, he returned. After bumbling around for a few more days, he called her and suggested a coffee. They met and he mumbled that he was maybe still in love with his ex and that he was REALLY sorry to do this to her. Mavis died a little bit inside and more or less never heard from him again; I plotted to find him and maim him in the eye area.

The Self-Startler is terrified of the one thing it looks like he really wants. Like a squirrel with a cashew phobia.

KEY CHARACTERISTICS

Here are some signs to look for that will help you identify a Self-Startler:

- He barrels in with impressive openers (like, 'I don't usually hit on women, but you have just changed that, I reckon', or, 'Now I know why

Joshua never introduced me to you – he wanted to keep you all to himself'), so that you instantly feel special.

- He lays on the compliments, but in an enticing manner. Makes you feel as though he really has never loved a laugh as much as he loves yours, or seen a girl carry off a yellow dress with such finesse, or met a girl who owns her own highly successful sex toy business.

- He's confident, mischievous and very forward, but in a non-sleazy manner. For example, on the first date he might ask if you'll be staying at his place – not for sex, just for making out – and you'll actually consider it, even though it goes against all your rules.

- He hounds you with cute, persistent texts, calls and emails for movies, dinner and other fun activities, to the point where you say yes just to shut him up.

- He creates a feeling of familiarity and 'Just go with the flow', so much so that you forget your lessons and start doing things like seeing him four nights a week (including one of those in tracksuit pants, eating Thai).

- He's a chronic long-term planner. Can't go a day, or a dinner, without suggesting another place he wants to take you for dinner, or a country the two of you should visit, or a friend or family member of his he can't wait for you to meet.

- He throws the L-bomb around like it's grain for chickens: 'I love the way you do your hair', or, 'I love spending Sundays in bed with you', or 'I love drinking Scotch with you after a meaty

game of backgammon'. He may even drop THE
L-bomb. The proper one. And after three weeks.

All of these things, you'll note, are pretty much in
direct contrast to what most guys do in the earliest
stages of dating. The long-term plans, the gushing, the
adoration, the familiarity ... This is precisely why
your ears should prick up, and your bushy little tail
should be stiff and alert. (You *are* a possum, right?)
Because, as women who have been sucked in by a Self-
Startler will tell you, if it looks, smells, sounds and
feels too good to be true, uh, it is.

Guys who do this already know it won't last, but it's like spending up big with the company credit card, knowing they're going bankrupt.

I know it's sad and it's cynical to write off a man
who barrels in spewing adoration, affection and a
heavy desire for commitment, as a man who is ultimately going to bail. I also know that it conflicts with
A LOT of what this book has told you, because I've
spent many hours thumping keys telling you that
a man needs to show you right from the outset that
he's keen, and that he needs to be persistent and open
about his feelings and blah blah blah.

BUT! There is a VAST, ASTRONOMICAL, MEGA,
GIGA difference between a man who is into you, and
a man who tells you 400 times a day he is into you.

Nescafé has known this for years. Too strong = bad.

If he is coming on too strong, he is coming on too
strong.

BEHAVIOURAL ANALYSIS

But *why* does he do this? What would inspire a man to
run into the arms of a woman with such fervour and
furious devotions of infatuation, romance-ification
and idolisation if he didn't really mean it?

Before we go any further, take a moment and consider whether you have ever rushed into something, be it a holiday, a new handbag, a job or even a decision about steak over fish, because at the time, you were feeling crazy, excitable or carefree. It probably doesn't happen too often – we women are meticulous about most of our decisions, which is code for the fact that we over-think and endlessly discuss things – but try to imagine that feeling of being impulsive and not thinking completely straight. Perhaps a time when you were fed up and just took any decision, or when you were feeling under-loved or low on self-esteem and that influenced your choices. You're beginning to understand the mindset of a man who sweeps you into an ocean of romance and then steals off in a dinghy in the middle of the night.

While it's difficult to imagine someone doing something as frivolous as this with another human being's emotions, it happens, doll. Here are a few reasons the Self-Startler bowls into your life with confetti and sirens, only to completely freak himself out when all of his magic starts to win your over.

1. He *loves* to chase-and-conquer, and will do anything to 'win'. Once he wins that challenge, he moves onto his next target.

2. He's just broken up with another woman, misses the deep physical and emotional bond they had and is trying to re-create it with you in 1/19th of the time.

3. He's smashing SERIOUS rebound-o-meters and you are the wall he has chosen to bounce off.

4. He is using you and your relationship (and this is direct from the Fucked-Up-But-True file) as

If he makes you Wear a Wig, that's a bit of a giveAway. →

ammunition against his ex, or a woman he *genuinely* likes. He needs her to see how totally into you he is for her to suddenly understand she's in love with him.

This is the dating equivalent of the thrill kill: he's doing it because he can. Like lions with disabled monkeys. Shame on you lion, that monkey still had a lot to live for.

Top Reasons a Self-Starter Startles Himself

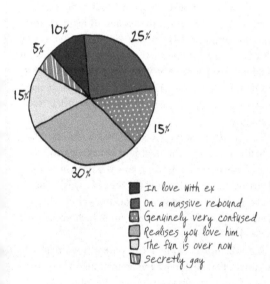

10%
5%
25%
15%
15%
30%

■ In love with ex
■ On a massive rebound
▦ Genuinely very confused
▨ Realises you love him
▢ The fun is over now
▩ Secretly gay

IT'S NOT ABOUT YOU

One girlfriend sadly got as far as being engaged to her Self-Startler, so when he bailed on her – citing the pace of how fast their relationship had progressed as the reason (interesting, considering he was the one who had set the dial to warp speed) – she was, understandably, an absolute mess. And to this day she has trouble trusting men who seem too nice, or too into her. Which is a REAL shame for those guys, who might be wonderful for all she knows.

Which brings me to this important piece of advice: *Don't take it personally!* It's not about you. The fact that he was telling you that he'd never felt this way about someone before, and that you were the capers in his puttanesca, the tequila in his margarita, the 100-watter in his kitchen ceiling, and then he fell off the face of the earth without so much as an email, DOESN'T MEAN YOU ARE NOT A CAPER, TEQUILA OR A LIGHT BULB. You're all of these things and a Quality Man will discover that soon enough.

Remember: you are deliciously salty, quite alcoholic, and have a small carbon footprint.

This time, you weren't dealing with a Quality Man.

Sadly, you were swindled into believing the hyperbole of a man who was using you as a prop in the play of his dysfunctional, confused life. He was a player of the most frustrating and shocking variety: he was delightful. And he sucked you in. Which sucks. Flat out sucks.

But take heart. No man can pursue a woman with this intensity if he doesn't genuinely think she is a Total Winner. No man can keep up that kind of façade. (Not even Tom Hanks, and did you see him in *Castaway*? I mean, that guy can *act*.)

Despite his leaving you reeling and writhing around in stunned confusion, with a deflated ego and disbelief that all of his actions and words led to nothing, take solace in the fact that deep down, he actually was very into you. He just went too far, too fast and freaked himself the fuck out. So on one hand, he pissed off the moment any of it was about to mean anything, but on the other hand, you had the pleasure and enjoyment of a guy beating down the door to hang out with you (and then avoided tying yourself down to a man with colossal issues).

Guys get like this because getting girls is like a game and you CAN get too addicted to the game, rather than the girl. But once you've got the girl (almost by accident), having a relationship's a different game altogether. And that's where it falls apart: we're rarely good at two games. (Me, for example: ping-pong - outstanding, water polo - disqualified for use of jet ski.)

6.

Men Don't Skip Footy Training For You

In this lesson, you'll learn the importance of keeping your friends, hobbies and social commitments while you're dating, and see the benefits this brings to you, him and your enjoyment of netball.

How often have you had an offer from the Guy You Like and have found yourself conflicted because you already had something planned for when he's asked you to go for a coffee/have dinner/see a movie/fly his remote-controlled plane? Next time you're in this situation, and you're thinking about cancelling or postponing that hairdresser appointment/catch-up with a friend/hot-air balloon ride, consider this: **men don't change or cancel their appointments for women.**

Have you ever asked a guy what he was doing that night, hoping to see him, and he's said, 'Well, I *did* have training on, but I guess I can skip it . . .'? No. You haven't. (If you have, quickly tattoo his name on your bicep, because he is a keeper.)

What you hear is, 'I've got training till 8.30 but I can see you after that . . .'. Or, 'I'm going for a quick

we operate our schedules on the first-in-best-dressed policy. Mostly because it requires too much effort to change things.

surf', or, 'I'm going round to Jamie's to fix his computer', or, 'I'm helping mum sew my sister's wedding dress'. Men keep their plans. They see no reason to cancel them. They know that they'll see you before or after. They don't panic. We can learn from them.

It's taken a while, but finally it's happened – something you can learn from us.

TAKE A TEST

1. You've been dating Jerry for five weeks. You really like him and want to see him every day. He calls you Saturday morning-ish – the day you'd locked in lunch and a walk with Bec and Megs – and asks if you want to have lunch and watch a movie. What do you say when he asks what you're doing today?
A. 'Well, I was going to go for lunch and a walk with the girls . . .'
B. 'I'm having lunch with the girls, then going for a walk.'
C. 'Going to see a movie with you, silly!'

2. Matt is a dreamboat but has an unpredictable job as a lion trainer, which means he often has to be spontaneous about your joint plans, because he has no phone service in the training cage. He calls you Tuesday at 5.30 and asks you to dinner. What do you say?
A. 'I'd love to but I've got netball . . . How about tomorrow?'
B. 'Ooh, gosh, I *usually* do yoga on Tuesdays . . .'
C. 'Will you be picking me up from work or home?'

D. 'I'll come to you.' WRONG! There are lions there! Come on, you're better than that. Stay on game.

3. You're at Julia's 30th having a walloping great time, doing your signature robot dance and drinking tequila from the bottle with all your best friends, but Patrick is starting to twitch and sit mute and hint at leaving.

With you. Together. This is one of your closest friend's big nights, it's only midnight and you *really* don't feel like going home. What do you say when he, gorgeous he, says, 'Come on babe, let's head'?

A. (Sigh.) 'Okay. Lemme get my bag.'

B. 'You know what? You go on ahead, I think I'm gonna stay a while longer.'

C. 'Staaaay. Come on . . . don't go. I want you to stay and dance and watch me do the worm.'

ANSWERS

1. Correct answer: B

Because you *are* going to lunch with the girls. And you can see him later. And because breaking plans with friends or family for no reason other than that a guy has called at the last minute to see if you're free is shitty behaviour.

> *Answered A?* You 'were going' to see the girls, but you're not now? The past tense has already given you away. He knows he's changed your plans. He knows he can call you with couple of hours notice and you'll drop plans that have probably been in place for a week. What kind of foundation is that setting up?

It starts here and next thing you know, he's combining your honeymoon with his end-of-season footy trip. And maybe not inviting you.

Answered C? Cool. Good for you. Just remember this next time you work your day around a plan you have with Natalie, and an hour out, when you're already dressed, she calls with some shithouse excuse as to why she has to pull out – and you know it's really because she's dumped you for pasta with a guy she's known for three minutes. Enjoy the movie!

2. Correct answer: A

You've engaged the apricot by sticking to your plans and

elegantly reminding him that you're not a 'last minute' kind of girl. It's not that you're not into spontaneity, *it's that you deserve more than two hours notice for dinner*. Spontaneity is not finishing work and thinking, 'I'd like to see her tonight. I'll call her and if she's busy I'll cover my inability to give her some notice by labelling it "spontaneity" rather than "disorganisation"'.

Answered B? There's that past tense language again. 'Usually' implies that's what you *would* do if he didn't make a better offer. Or any offer, by the sounds of things. Even one involving contracting malaria, just for fun.

Answered C? I'm sure that your burritos will be delightful. It's the long-term learning I'm more concerned with. What on earth would ever make him change this behaviour? Nothin'. That's what.

3. Correct answer: B

Good move. *Clever move.* You're having fun, you don't want to leave; *he* does. You're not conjoined twins, so he goes, you stay. You mustn't feel bad or guilty. You're honouring something that was important in your life well before he walked onto the scene, and he won't be pissed off about that (or shouldn't be). In fact, I think he'll be both quietly impressed that you stood your ground and just that little bit more attracted to you. After all, you have told him that your friends – and your desire to dance around a handbag in a nightclub with them at 1 a.m. – are important to you, and he can't change that just by uttering a 'Babe, wanna go?' Compare this to the girl who grabs her coat and exits the moment he suggests leaving. Which would you prefer: having him go to bed wondering what you're doing and what time you'll be home, and if you'll be staying at his place or not, or having him going to bed smug that you are pretty much wrapped around his finger? Exactly.

Answered A? So, you're leaving. Okay. Let's just get a little perspective for a moment. You've known the birthday girl for how long? Six years. And how many times has she turned 30 in that time? Just once? I see. Well, I guess it's not *that* big a deal then. I'm sure she won't even notice you've gone, and she certainly won't be at all offended, not for one nanosecond, that you left with a guy you've known for less than six weeks because he's tired and a little bored.

Answered C? Good for you. Do ask him to stay a little while longer. Let him know this is important to you and that if you're having fun, then you're probably not going to stop having fun just because your date wants to go home. If he still wants to leave, or stays but is obviously zapping your mojo, kiss him and gently push him out the door with a mischievous spank on the bot bot. He won't mind. He'll still exist tomorrow and you can go get a bacon and egg roll together and tell him about all of the magnificent freestyle worming you did.

Plus doing the worm gives you nine bonus attraction points.

WHAT HAVE YOU LEARNED?

When you stand your ground and reject his requests or last-minute invites, you're doing the right thing by *you*. And I don't think I can stress enough how important it is to be looking after yourself first when laying the foundations of a Quality Relationship. Hang on, maybe I can: *VERY IMPORTANT.*

Knocking him back every now and then is nothing you need to overanalyse, or feel guilty about. A woman who can keep that sweet, sweet (and fucking difficult sometimes) quality of respecting the friends, engagements, and activities she had in place before the guy came along is much more attractive than the one who happily kicks her life to the curb in favour of the one he's creating.

Some women freak out at the idea of turning down the guy they're dating. They mistakenly believe he'll never ask again or he'll think she doesn't like him. But know this (and know it well, because it is one of those lessons that inspire conflict between the head and the heart): **None of this behaviour will offend him or make you seem like 'a bitch' or hard work.** In fact, it will gain you respect, and (consciously or subconsciously) he'll recognise that you're not someone who devalues herself, her friends or her family, and when you commit to something, you mean it. Clever men will see that not as a threat, but as the promise of a really excellent relationship. He gets to keep his poker nights and footy; she gets to keep her massages and erotic pottery class. Happy times!

It's also worth remembering: rejection is the sweetest aphrodisiac. Every time you reject him, he feels a little twinge of ouch and surprise. Swiftly followed by a little growl of 'I must make her mine'. And if he backs off? Re-read Module One, Lesson 7. If he can't accept that the very things that attracted him to you in the first place (your sense of fun, your friendship circle, your dedication to kickboxing, your dog-walking business) will be staying in place, he's not only confused but delusional, because if there is one thing guys dislike, it's when their girlfriends give up their lives for their relationship.

In fact, knowing we're not being relied upon as 'sole source of happiness' is a massive relief. Like, if you ran the only chocolate store in town, you'd never feel like you could take a day off. Certainly not 'round Easter.

7.

Be Too Much of a Man and Lose the Man

In this lesson, you'll learn that what we do has more impact than we realise on the men we date. This is especially salient when we want men to know we're interested, but we're trying to create meaningful relationship boundaries.

Despite the fact that they obviously have some of the finest and most biased relationship advice on tap at all times, amazingly some of my friends still mess up and act all human and shit. And there are rumours that *I do too*. (I know. I couldn't believe it at first either.)

And in which area do my friends and I drop the ball? Being honest with our feelings and communication. Being mindful that if we play the man too much, we can lose the man. Being aware that all that self-protective armour needs to come off at some point.

FIELD REPORT

Take my friend Jemima. We had many, many conversations about her relationship and finally recognised that, possibly, she wasn't going about it in the best way. Some background: Jemima was happy and social, loved her work, and was dating a lovely man called Gilbert. Gilbert wanted to see her all the time, he had no issue indicating that he was keen, and he didn't even appear to be a Self-Startler. Gilbert was pretty swell! But sometimes Jemima felt he didn't respond in the way he was 'supposed to'. Sometimes, when she would tell him she was busy all week, he would say 'no worries', but would later seem annoyed. Or when she would say she was dead keen on moving to London next year, he would become quiet. Finally, after six months, Gilbert said that he felt like Jemima constantly reminded him she didn't need him and that it was becoming tired. Jemima spluttered that she shouldn't be chastised for living her life, especially since that was what attracted him in the first place. Gilbert said he understood that she wanted to maintain her independent woman stance, and he respected and admired that, but he could only endure miss so-busy-playing-hardball for so long.

Jemima called me in tears, very confused: she thought she was doing all the Right Things, and now they were putting her in danger of losing Great Gilbert! What was she supposed to do? She wasn't even sure what was right anymore.

Jemima has valid concerns, and her situation is extremely common. And if, like Jemima, you've come this far and you're starting to feel confused, agitated and kind of shitty at me for writing this stupid fucking book in the first place, because life was easier when you were just doing what you were doing, you are NOT ALONE. But know that you are absolutely on the right path, and that you are taking the right steps,

Hamish's guess: Gilbert, like all guys, is like a cactus — Whilst he can survive without water for ages, he still needs a little bit. (Jemima's love is the water.)

and while it may not be easy, or infallible, you're generating a dazzling core of self-confidence and rebuilding yourself in preparation for a Quality Relationship.

RETAIN THE LOVE

A lot of us struggle with the shift that is required when you start putting your needs, time and wants before that of a man's – having to actively hold yourself back from doing what you have unthinkingly done for years, whether that's calling him whenever you feel like it, or seeing him every time he asks you, or moving to Sweden to help him run his massage school.

The lessons in this book are asking you to have faith in something that feels incredibly difficult and foreign, on top of teaching you to break habits you have had for many years. Switching mindsets can be especially difficult if you are torn between being a Life's Too Short person and wanting to be a Chase person, or your heart is saying, 'See him a lot or he will lose interest!' and your brain is commanding that you, 'Control the pace and reap the long-term benefits!'

you're in real trouble if your other organs start yelling too. Quiet, spleen!

But here's the thing. *You are trying to break your old habits because they weren't serving you.* You're reading this book because you felt you needed to realign your emotional landscape and regain some control in an area of your life that has baffled or constantly disappointed you.

Here are some things to remember when you are finding yourself frustrated, or confused, or hands-thrown-up-in-the-airy:

- What you're trying to do, and the reasons for trying to do it, *drip* with courage and self-love.

- Adopting some form of strategy is crucial when you are trying to make changes to longstanding practices.
- Nothing easily won is appreciated.
- Men respond favourably to challenges.
- Putting yourself first is not a Bad Thing.
- You're hot and cool and you're wearing really great shoes.

Part of Jemima's concern is that she *thought* she was doing all the right things, and, for all intents and purposes, she was. However, something is missing. By all means show a man you are an independent, self-respecting woman who doesn't drop everything for a guy, but please remember to *do it with love*. Do it with a sense of softness (engage that apricot), retain a sense of kindness and refrain from playing games for the sake of playing games. You are doing this because you're tired of being hurt . . . so why turn around and hurt someone else?

Oh, come now. Scrape your jaw off the floor and unknit those cranky little eyebrows. I'm not going back on everything I have said up until this point. (Did I write: *Call him back as soon as he calls you! Say yes to every date he asks you on! Start leaving clothes at his place after the fifth date!* No.) The whole manifesto of this book is that you need to look after yourself and love yourself before you can love others. When this self-love is genuine, you don't need to constantly prove that it exists.

Whether it's because of the guy you've been dating, or simply because the seams that hold together your resolve, focus and outlook on relationships are

you don't have to believe everything you read in brackets. (I live in a ham igloo.)

unravelling, you need to sit back and take a moment to consider not only why you're doing this, but *how* you're doing it. Are you confusing emotional nonchalance with a genuine wish to take your time when it comes to love? Are you scared he'll run when you start to soften and become your true, loving, adoring self? Is your head battling your heart with a large baton?

We all go through this.

It's completely normal. I have turned away several Good Men because I took my Super Giga Beyoncé Single Foxy Power Woman thing just that little bit too far. It's easy to do. So be careful and learn from my mistakes.

HAVE YOU GONE TOO FAR?

Here are some signs you might be taking *your* Super Giga Beyoncé Single Foxy Power Woman manifesto a little too far:

- **You've crossed that fine line of being self-sufficient and started being self-centred.** He asks you to go to dinner and you agree. But then you accidentally go out and drink 36 shots the night before, and you're lounge-locked and vomity on the day of the date. Self-sufficient girl calls him, laughs about how she feels and suggests a lo-fi date instead. Selfish girl texts him and says she's not feeling well and needs to cancel.

- **You mistake putting your needs first with your needs being the only ones that are important.** He wants to stay out because it's his brother's engagement party, but you want to go home because you have an early start. You *could* view

this as the perfect opportunity to set a bound-
ary that you don't have to do as he does, and
that you can trot off home whenever you feel
like it . . . Or you could stay and hang out with
him because he really wants you to, and it would
mean a lot to him. The longer you date a guy, the
more your mind should be drifting towards the
latter option.

- **You feel you have to prove your point all the
time, even when doing so is inconvenient or contrived.** You really want to go out with him for a
few drinks on Saturday night, but he's feeling a
little exhausted. You go out anyway with a girlfriend to prove a point, even though you really
only wanted to be with him and don't actually
enjoy yourself.

- **You're so devoted to maintaining your fun, busy,
awesome social life that he starts to feel that not
only do you not have time for him, you don't
even *want* to make time for him.** He asks when
he can see you this week and you fire back an
SMS saying, 'It's a busy one, will text you tomo
when I have a better idea x'.   ←

To be honest, we'd be consoled by the 'x' and play Xbox, but I see what you're saying.

This seems to be the murky little pool Jemima found
herself in. It's the stage where you have put him
through The Chase and the persistence test, and he
passed, and now that the two of you are navigating
your way through the dating maze, a considered decision on your behalf as to where this whole thing is
going is needed. You need to stop for a moment and
evaluate just how and why you are behaving the way
you are, and if it's likely to keep him interested and

attracted to you (good), or just piss him off and send him packing (bad).

And they do piss off! *They piss off a lot!* Think about it: from his perspective he has done the hard yards, he has pursued you valiantly, convinced you that he is a Good Guy, and has successfully enticed you into spending some enjoyable time with him, at cafés and bars, on sofas and in the boudoir. And sure, your full life and independence was a large part of the reason that he went to these lengths, but there comes a time when you have to gently merge into more of a duet, and less of a solo performance.

Even if you just let us sing backup vocals, we're usually pretty happy with that.

Of course, if you are yet to have the 'Being Exclusive' chat (see Module Two, Lesson 9), there is no mutual agreement of the two of you being a couple yet, so, in theory, you're both still free to do your own little thing, date other people, whatever.

But. With each progressive dinner, and movie, and coffee, and sleepover, you have to understand that the 'relationship', or whatever it is at this point, advances a little bit. He learns a little more about you, and you about him. He decides he likes you a little bit more, and you decide the same about him.

Remember: If you sell us 'I don't need a man' too hard, we'll eventually buy it and go off to find a girl who gives us, 'I may need a man, but you have to try bloody hard'. which is less concise but more appealing.

So, if you want him to stick around, you need to be mindful of this. This doesn't mean suddenly seeing him five nights a week, or falling over yourself to let him know how much you adore him. It means finetuning your full and exciting Super Giga Beyoncé Single Foxy Power Woman I-don't-need-a-man-to-be-happy manifesto and lifestyle into something a little softer and encouraging for a man who, for all intents and purposes, *has earned it.*

COMMON SIGNALS WHICH WILL PUSH MEN AWAY

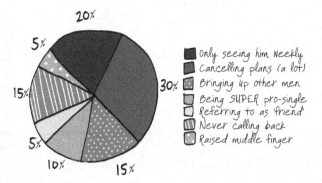

20%

5%

5%

15%

5%

10%

15%

30%

- Only seeing him weekly
- Cancelling plans (a lot)
- Bringing up other men
- Being SUPER pro-single
- Referring to as 'friend'
- Never calling back
- Raised middle finger

CHECKLIST

Reassessing your mindset at this crossroad is imperative. See how you answer these questions, which will assist you in being clear about the signals you're sending him. If he's starting to lose interest in you, or isn't calling as much, perhaps you aren't throwing off happy-cool-single-woman vibes, but rather I-don't-need-or-want-a-boyfriend-so-you-are-probably-wasting-your-time vibes. There's a fine line. Walk it with teeny little ballet slippers and a harness.

- Are you trying to convince yourself you don't need him?
- Are you trying to convince *him* you don't need him?
- Do you genuinely like him, and you're forcing yourself to play cool so as to keep him keen?

- Are your actions and responses less cute and carefree, and more actually offensive?
- How would you feel if he was behaving towards you the way you are to him?
- Are you scared that if you soften up, he'll lose interest?
- Are you totally in love with Robert Pattinson, like I am?

Heck yes.

8.

If He Hands You Lemons, *Don't* Make Him a Gin and Tonic

In this lesson, you'll learn that if you find yourself making excuses for a man – verbally or internally, minor or massively major – you should stop and assess whether he's worth it. You might have to face up to the fact that he's just not Trying Very Hard.

When a guy you're seeing suggests catching up for a drink one night, undertaking to call you at lunch to plan it, and then by 7 p.m. you've heard nothing, you're probably (rightly) pretty pissed off. You could have gone to the movies with your sister, or to dinner with Pete and Sam, or many other awesome options, but now you're wedged into that the revolting Phone Checking State where you *really* want to see this guy, but you don't want to contact him (he said he'd call *you* and you shouldn't have to remind him that he wanted to see you).

And yet, when you speak to your friend that

evening, and she asks why you're not making out with him in the back of his car, you find yourself saying things like, 'It wasn't a concrete plan, it was just an idea, so no drama,' or, 'Well, he didn't say what time exactly . . . I'm sure he just got tied up and he'll call in a bit.'

And sure, this scenario may *sound* relatively normal, not that big a deal, and nothing to get all Self-Helpy High-Horsey about. But it is, because while he may have had legit reasons for his behaviour, and you may genuinely have been okay about not getting your date, his actions demonstrate that:

1. He is Not Trying Very Hard.
2. You have morphed into an Excusinator.

Tip: If he's treating you worse than his mates, something is wrong with the set-up.

Both of which, on the scale of great to ungreat, sit right up the ungreat end, next to being stood up and finding out he used to sleep with that Kelly moll you hate.

HE'S NOT TRYING VERY HARD

By this stage – of the textbook and of your dating life – you should be able to spot very quickly if he's Not Trying Very Hard. If he's not calling or texting when he said he would, or he's breaking dates, or making excuses, or leaving you frustrated and dejected on designated date night, or causing you to make excuses, he's Not Trying Very Hard to indicate to you that, in the constellation of men that make up the male species, he stands out as a shining star, and is the one over ALL the others you should be with. In fact, by the sounds of his behaviour, it almost sounds like he's

Trying Very Hard to prove to you that he is NOT the
one you should be with.

IT TAKES 23 SECONDS TO SEND A
TEXT MESSAGE

Of all my relationship advice, this is the message I
seem to find myself dispensing the most, and which I
stand by passionately. It's generally hauled out when
I see a girlfriend doing her head in over a guy who
hasn't contacted her when he said he would, or when
he should have done by now. Or he's due to respond to
her text, or has fallen off the face of the earth into the
Boy Black Hole, where none of the mobile phone net-
works work, but luckily no one notices because there
is plenty of beer and pool.

It's this: **it takes 23 seconds to send a text message.**
If your guy can't find less than half a minute to send
you a message, to update you on his plans when he'd
made you think you were to be part of them, or to tell
you he's busy, or that he went for an all-day surf up the
coast, or to let you know his flight gets in at 7 . . . then
how much can he honestly think of you?

Think of it this way: if *you* had a semi-plan with
The Guy You're Dating in place, but you realised at
the eleventh hour that you weren't going to be able to
make it after all – maybe your dinner or lunch has run
over – you'd fire off a little text to let him know as soon
as you could. Wouldn't you? And if for some reason you
had no battery left in your phone, you would probably
borrow someone else's. Because you know it's a shitty
thing to do to leave another human being hanging.

It comes down to respect and courtesy. And if your

This is where guys are trying to find out what they can get away with and yet not get into trouble. Like sneaking through sillier and sillier deductions on your tax return each year.

what? where is this pl—? oh. I see. Sarcasm

dude can't swing you a little bit of that when you're dating, what makes you think he'll suddenly start streaming it once he knows you're 100% his? Or that he's more than casually interested? It sounds to me like he's Not Trying Very Hard. In which case, he's wasting your time.

Or, put another way: 'Jerks are jerks, so don't date jerks.'

DATING DICTIONARY: EXCUSINATOR

An Excusinator is someone who (sometimes sub-consciously) makes excuses for people who don't deserve it. Excusinators are common in the dating environment, especially among women, who tend to talk up dates and New Guys to the point of conver-sational saturation. (Technical term: Mentionitis.) Their unproven man suddenly finds himself on a ped-estal that, quite frankly, he hasn't earned. Generally, after all that talk-up, if the New Guy lets his dating co-star down in a dating/phone call situation, women feel incredibly exposed and can quickly spin a web of excuses to make sure neither they nor the New Guy come away looking bad. Unfortunately, this veils the true meaning of the situation, which is that he is Not Trying Very Hard.

Tip: Excusinators are not robots who promise to travel back in time to kill Sarah Connor but, when they get there, chicken out and say they have robo-measles.

THE BIGGER PICTURE

Making small excuses for his behaviour when you're dating can morph into *big-time* excuse-making for his behaviour when you move on to making it an exclu-sive relationship. Here's what that might look like:

- He's the guy that says he's staying over after 'a

few quiet beers first' at 7.15 p.m. on a Wednesday night. By 2.23 a.m., when he's not home and hasn't contacted you, you're frothing. Not because he's out, but because it doesn't occur to him to let you know that he's decided to *stay* out, and now you can't sleep because your ears prick up at the sound of every car that pulls into the street.

- He forgets important dates and doesn't really honour those he does remember, because when you were dating you told yourself (and others) it didn't bother you.

- He doesn't bother to make an effort (conversational or otherwise) with your friends or family, because when you were first dating you let it slide that he was a complete social handbrake.

- He goes on all-weekend benders, loosely alerting you on Thursday to the fact he won't be in contact (or thinking about you), by saying things like, 'Have a good weekend'.

- He constantly tells you he'll buy you a yacht, but keeps buying you diamonds and Italian sports cars instead.

HANDY HINT

You teach people how they should treat you! So please ensure you do it from the very beginning. The moment you begin dating a man is the moment you begin teaching him how you like to be treated. He'll be doing the same, giving you little 'tests' and seeing how far he can push his luck – even if he doesn't know he's doing it – so fair is fair.

WHAT HAVE YOU LEARNED?

You can't *make* a man treat you the way you want him to. But you can *find* a man who will. Men arrive on your doorstep the way they are, and this very, very, VERY rarely changes. Please don't fall into that big sinkhole of bullshit that tricks you into thinking once you find a guy, you can change him. *You can't.* (See Module Three, Lesson 2.) However, you *can* demonstrate to him what you will and won't accept in a relationship, and see if he's willing to play along. Of course, he's completely within his rights to do the same to you. Which means that if his sacred Friday footy nights are a deal breaker, you have to deal. It's a two-way expressway.*

*To Love Town.

Don't forget that in the dating stages, the Guy You're Dating should be putting on a good show. If he can't manage to be respectful and courteous (which obviously you are to him) in this Peacocking Stage, then you can pretty much guarantee he won't suddenly become Guy of The Year when you move into a Proper Relationship with him.

To be treated like a queen, you have to be dealing with a king.

Bonus analogy extension: If he only vaguely looks like a king but has a slightly different hat on, he's a joker.

And if he's *Not* Trying Very Hard, he's not the King you're looking for – he's lazy, or he's displaying the classic signs of About to Abort. You don't have to put up with it, and you shouldn't find yourself making excuses for him. Don't waste precious months or even years making the best of a bad situation. Go find a good one instead.

9.

Becoming Exclusive and the RDC

In this lesson, you'll learn the art of recognising when 'the talk' about Being Exclusive should happen, how to instigate it and why it's such an important conversation.

While it would be preferable to explain romantic relationships as our friends in Hollywood do (fantastical, convenient, predictable/predictably unpredictable), unfortunately it's a little more complex that that. Sadly, we don't all have best friends that we will end up falling in love with just as we are perched on the church steps, on the way to say 'I do' to someone else.

Still, sometimes you're treated to a single defining moment where you realise you absolutely, definitely want to be with this person, and they feel it too, and it all happens during a fight over that stupid girl at his work who you secretly think he's screwing, only he's *not*, because he only wants to be with you, and then you're kissing and it's decided that you're now in an exclusive relationship (and the music comes up, the camera spirals into the trees and the credits roll).

*This is as big as we'll ever go, if we're being honest. Any more is like paying $10000 more than you needed to on a car, 'just to be sure'.

And sometimes the guy you're dating professes his love and tells you he wants to 'give this thing a go',* and you know exactly where he stands on things, and it's so deliciously easy that you can't help feeling smug when you read this chapter, because NONE OF IT APPLIES TO YOU.

Whatever, Smuggy. Why don't you go have a lie-down on your Persian smug.

Fairytale beginnings aside, mostly the way things pan out is that we begin to find ourselves at a stage of dating when suddenly it doesn't feel like enough. You want more. You may even start to feel indignant: 'Dammit, after four months I *deserve* to meet his parents.' Or: 'Would it kill him to leave some spare clothes at my place?' Or: 'When is he going to drop the L-bomb?' That kind of caper. You can't decide if you should be introducing him as Your Boyfriend, or you become offended that he isn't introducing you as his girlfriend, and that leads you to wonder if you two are going to take this thing to the next level anytime soon. (Suffice to say, if you're thinking along these lines it's fairly safe to assume you're into him and *you* want things to progress. If, on the other hand, when he refers to you as his girlfriend you have to hold down a little bit of vomit from entering your mouth, it's probably not a great sign.)

Sometimes the realisation that you want to 'go steady' will be catalyst-driven: perhaps he is going overseas for three weeks and you're not sure if you're allowed to date or kiss other men during that time, or if he will be sexing women in Bali (and you'd be a fool for thinking he wouldn't just because the two of you have been dating). You'll be wondering if the two of you should be having the RDC (Relationship Defining Chat), and much energy and girlfriend-discussion will be consumed with how exactly you can bring up your feelings without scaring him off.

What all of this comes down to is that at some stage in the extended dating process, some formal labels will be required. These labels will generally be decided upon during an RDC, which, by law, must occur before two people dating can segue into the world of a Relationship – otherwise known as shifting from Casual Dating into Being Exclusive.

DATING DICTIONARY: BEING EXCLUSIVE

I realise how American-teen-movie this term is, but Being Exclusive is the simplest way to describe the commitment of being solely in a relationship with one other person. Being Exclusive means you don't date anyone else and that you have moved on from just dating each other to being in a fully-fledged relationship. In ye olde days, it was kind of assumed that once you started sleeping with someone, you were exclusive. But these days, it's not so black and white. It's more amethyst with flecks of emerald and magenta. People often date several people at once, and while *you* might be savvy enough to realise that you can only do that if you're not sleeping with any of them (or just one, the one you really like), you can't assume everyone else is on the same wavelength. (See 'Multi-dating and Sexual Exclusivity', page 154.)

When you become exclusive, there is an agreement that the two of you are going to give this thing a shot,

worth knowing: Guys love the idea of frolicking unhitched through the countryside forever, but also know it can't last, and do actually _want_ the RDC. (Mostly because we usually sense we're in a relationship well before we admit to ourselves we've been tamed.)

and that maybe one day you might even exchange rings, have babies and buy houses and shit. Otherwise, *why bother?* If either of you thought the other one wasn't sufficiently aligned in terms of values, desires, general outlook on life and kinky bedroom moves, then you wouldn't bother shifting out of dating into exclusivity.

By Being Exclusive, you're admitting that you have chosen this person over all the others, which must mean they are pretty special. (And considering how hard we make it for men to get to this level, he MUST be good.)

There are expectations of each other's behaviour that accompany Being Exclusive, which are different for every relationship and which you'll need to delicately negotiate. These exist both as a way to set boundaries and to ensure you're on the same page. Your expectations might range from an agreement that you won't pash on with that Martin guy anymore when you're drunk and lonely, or that you'll see each other at least a few times a week. Maybe it's that he won't Facebook flirtatiously with that Eliza bird anymore. Maybe it's that when one of you is invited to a party or wedding, the other is also invited, or that you can now introduce each other as 'girlfriend' or 'boyfriend'. Maybe it's that you don't talk about your relationship with your friends, or that toothbrushes may now be left at the other's place. It might even come down to laying down the law: for example, that a kiss is counted as infidelity; or that a kiss isn't included as infidelity, but sex is. That email flirting with workmates is not on. And so on.

It's a chance for both of you to air your needs for a happy, healthy relationship. And in most cases, the only chance: it's futile trying to set up expectations midway through a relationship: established behaviour patterns are almost impossible to break. If you don't do this now, and something upsetting happens, one party is usually so distressed that the other didn't *immediately* know that what they were doing was hurtful, that the result is fighting, disbelief, anger and the immediate switching of Facebook status from *In a Relationship* to *It's Complicated*.

Have you ever blown up at your partner when you found out that he caught up with an ex, and his response was that he didn't know it would upset you? Exactly. Having a mutual understanding of what's offensive, even if it feels a bit wrong and like you're at school, pays itself off in peace of mind in the long run.

Just be gentle, because this dog has been unleashed for a while and may scratch a bit.

MULTI-DATING AND SEXUAL EXCLUSIVITY

There is a vast difference between Being Exclusive and having an exclusive *sexual relationship* with someone. If you're dating a guy, pre-RDC, then technically, since you haven't defined your relationship as Being Exclusive, you – and he – can still date others. *However.* I strongly advise being *sexually* exclusive with one guy you're dating at a time – the one you're *really* into, the one you're hoping to be fully exclusive with. By all means, until the two of you have openly stated that you're only going to see each other, date other dudes, but my recommendation is not to sleep with them.

It feels a little bit obvious to state why, but in my opinion sleeping with multiple men is probably not going to offer any great clarity or feelings of

The other dudes will evaporate as sure as water ... evaporates. zing!

self-fulfilment. What it probably *will* do is confuse you and cloud your judgement. And just as you're probably not going to be thrilled to find out your Main Guy has been sleeping with other women while dating you, you can be pretty sure he won't be ecstatic to find out you were schtooping other dudes while dating *him*. Just sayin'.

THE RDC (RELATIONSHIP DEFINING CHAT)

Dating can be a wild, pothole-filled little road, which is why you both need to be clear about where you stand on it. There's no good you sitting happily perched atop the 110 sign if he's holding up a whopping great stop sign, for example. You both need to be honest about where it's all heading (man, this road analogy was *made* for me) and how you'll be travelling. The RDC is precisely for this purpose. It is intended to get the two of you talking, no matter how briefly and awkwardly (it could be over in a few minutes, a blip on your conversational radar on the way to dinner), about where you both think this relationship is heading, or where you want it to head. Are you both happy to move from dating to Being Exclusive? Or is he not sure?* Are you not sure? Are you both happy with things the way they are? Are you prepared to walk if he's not willing to kick things up a gear? I know, I know – even writing those sentences inspired several thousand men worldwide to start running. But the RDC has gotta happen. Because unfortunately, a relationship that hasn't been defined is like a bottle of tomato sauce – not a relationship at all.

*He will be – why give up freedom?

But great with mini sausage rolls.

WHEN TO HAVE THE RDC

The RDC is due when you're feeling a little bit unsure of where it's all heading with this guy you've been dating for some time. When you want to call him at the end of the day, 'just because', but you're not sure if that's cool, or if he's with some other girl and you'll look like a tool. When you're frustrated with what you feel to be stagnation. When you keep finding yourself wanting to say, 'I love you', but holding back. When you really like him and he has given you all the indications that he feels the same way. It's normal to be nervous about this chat. Nerves are good! They demonstrate that you feel something for this guy, that he has shown you he is a winner.

Remember: He's just as nervous as you. Like when you confront a cow in the wild.

Don't forget that this intermission between courting and an exclusive relationship is often clouded by insecurity. You're both wondering how the other is feeling (or at least you are, to be considering the RDC) – do they like you enough to be exclusive, and are they seeing anybody else, and . . . Look, it can be fucking nerve-racking, to be blunt. But in the big scale of things, it's fleeting. And besides, it's all part of the fun and excitement and dizziness of finding someone awesome.

Now, while I would love – *love* – to say here that you can chillax, 'cause this transition from dating to Being Exclusive will just happen organically in these modern times (and when you're too old to pass him a scrap of paper saying, 'Will you be my girlfriend? Tick yes or no'), I'm afraid it needs to be actively instigated. And if he's not doing it, sugar, then you need to.

HOW TO INSTIGATE THE RDC

Okay, so obviously you've decided something needs to be said. You and He need to sort out whether you're taking this boat into the harbour of Relationship Town, or if it's going to drift out to sea and hit an iceberg and snap into two separate parts.

A friend, May, asked me how she should kick off the RDC recently, because she was pretty sure that the arsehole/Best Guy Ever she was seeing was hooking up with this girl he had a history with, and she wanted to know if it was true. She felt the talk would be a good way to ascertain if: a) He had been cheating on her with this girl; and more importantly, b) If it could be even *considered* cheating, because she wasn't sure if they were an item yet.

Her point was valid: it was a good time to instigate the talk. She had a right to know. Here are some other times you should (sneakily) instigate the RDC:

- He's into you and he's doing all the right things to show you.
- You no longer want to date/sleep with other guys.
- You feel like he isn't into you.
- You're not into him.
- You text each other before bed each night, if you haven't already called each other, or are in each other's arms.
- You're seeing each other four times a week plus.
- He says little things that indicate he'd be jealous or offended if he saw you on a date with another dude. For example: 'So, do you come here with all your boyfriends?' Or: 'If no other man is taking you to dinner on Friday night, I'd love to.'

Or, after you go out with the girls on a Saturday night, he says: 'So, did you pick up?', or 'If you were dating anyone else I would be forced to hunt them down and seriously maim them'.

- He invites you to functions and you ask if you can bring him as a date to a friend's wedding.
- One of you is about to go away for an extended period and there's some uncertainty as to the rules of engagement during this period.
- You're dating two other guys and know that you aren't serious about ANY of them, this guy included.
- You're wasting his time.
- He's wasting yours.

But most of the time, you will just know.

Choose a time when you're both mellow (not code for smashed) and having a bit of a chat already. I advise using a playful frame for the conversation if possible, a technique that uses humour to dilute the 'heaviness' and awkwardness of the topic.

Simple, cheeky ways to engage the topic include:

- 'So, what do you tell your friends about us?'
- 'So, while you're in Tokyo, am I allowed to take up Eugene from IT on his offer of a *Star Wars* DVD marathon?'
- 'So, um, my ex called yesterday and wanted to catch up. I told him it would be inappropriate considering . . . well, you know, that we're . . . seeing each other . . .'
- 'Kel was asking how you were the other day. She adores you, as you know, and she said, "So are you two, like, boyfriend and girlfriend or

what?", and it occurred to me that I didn't quite know . . .'

- 'Do you want to marry me? You pretty much want to marry me, don't you . . .' (Note: I'm kidding. Don't actually propose to him.)

you'll know he's realised it's the RDC when a thin film of sweat appears over his body. In his head, the part of him that wants a relationship is firing up and the part that still wants to be on schoolies is screaming.

At the very least, this kind of conversational whitebait should get the two of you talking about your relationship to the point where you can ascertain if you're on the same page. It will require a little bit of boldness and vulnerability from both of you. For example, you might need to admit that you're either not ready to go any further, or that you would be hurt if you saw him out at dinner with another girl; he might need to reveal he wants to punch walls when he hears that your ex has been calling you, or that he is in love with the woman who serves him at his local café.

If you're anything like me, you'll freak out a little bit at the idea of this. Especially if you're keen to dance on into a relationship with him. After all, have you not just spent the last couple of months being busy, single, fabulous and deliberately non-committal? Yes. But that stuff was important at *that* stage, just as this stuff is important now.

POSSIBLE OUTCOMES OF THE RDC

He wants to move ahead, but you don't

This might feel suspiciously like a break-up conversation, but it shouldn't. Yes, you have been dating for a little while, and yes, you may have been sexually exclusive with this guy, but you don't need to feel like an arsehole for telling him that you've decided you'd rather keep your 'options open', or that you're 'just not ready for a relationship right now'. Be honest. It's far better to be honest with him about how you feel than for you to keep on seeing him, and have him thinking he's a whisker away from entering a Quality Relationship. Flip the script and imagine how you would feel.

He's happy with the way things are, but you want to move ahead

Ooh, this one is a bit ouchy. Especially if you feel he's given you all the signals that he's into you. You need to apply some BRUTAL honesty in this situation. Can you pretend to be happy with how things are knowing that he has no intention, at this point anyway, of making you his Exclusive Girlfriend? Could you handle the idea that he, likely as not, will see other women as well as you? My recommendation is obviously to *rack off*. You want different things, and if he doesn't want to be exclusive with you, it means that he wants to be non-exclusive with several women. This can only lead to emotional torture.

He may also be testing what he can he can get away with ... again. You might have to use the 'U' word to shove him into reality. ('Ultimatum', not 'uranium'. Although that would shock him.)

He's happy with the way things are, and so are you

Good for you! You're a totally in-sync couple. You should be morning TV show hosts or something. This result may come about because the talk was a teeny bit premature (nothing wrong with that), or because while you like each other, you're both happy to just date non-exclusively for now, and you're okay with the idea that you each might date other people. Look, I can't help thinking that this is code for 'not serious', or 'headed for doom' – but there's nothing wrong with that. You'll just have another RDC in a little while. (See 'Disclaimers', opposite.)

He wants to move ahead, and so do you
Unfurl the sails! We have a relationship on our hands! You both like each other, you're not cool with either of you seeing other people, you're both prepared to deal with each other's families and friends (even when you're hung-over and REALLY couldn't be arsed), and whoever initiated the RDC was correct to do so. Sound the siren: the land of Exclusivity has two new members.

HIGHLY RECOMMENDED EXTRA RDC QUESTION

'Honey, so maybe, while we're talking about . . . stuff . . . Is there anything – aside from me sleeping with your brother – that you would *not* be cool with in this relationship?'

This may be the only chance you have to communicate (gently) what your relationship boundaries are. This is the time to tell him you're fine with him having Rebecca as a friend, but that you'd feel uncomfortable if you found out they went out to dinner or drinks, just the two of them. Or that you really value your relationship with your ex before your ex, and that there is NOTHING going on, and you'd still like to see him occasionally. Or that a kiss is definitely counted as cheating. That kind of thing.

I'm not suggesting you roll out a four-page document of rules (or *am* I . . .?). Just mention anything you feel strongly about and that you're not sure he's aware of, but which could lead to unhappiness, fights, break-ups and, in extreme cases, water bombs and rotten eggs being thrown.

DISCLAIMERS

Sometimes it will not be as clear-cut as this. Emotions sometimes selfishly don't behave in predictable ways, and it has been the case on occasion that you think you don't want to be exclusive with a guy, and then he tells you he doesn't either, and then you realise that you actually DO want to be exclusive with him. (Sicko.)

Some guys are One-Women Men, and they want to lock you in as soon as decide they like you and they feel you like them. This is good in as much as you're sure he's not playing the proverbial, and in that he will instigate the RDC (probably daily until he wins you over). Just be sure he's not a Self-Startler (Module Two, Lesson 5) or a compulsive liar before you dive in.

If you both say you're happy with the way things are, one of you is going to end up hurt. You can't dance around non-commitment land forever – eventually a decision has to be made on whether you're going to go your separate ways, or whether you're going to give it a nudge. That's why you had the RDC in the first place, remember? God, didn't *anyone* pay attention to what happened with Samantha and that smooth hotel-owner guy on *Sex and the City*?

WHAT HAVE YOU LEARNED?

Well, lots, hopefully. Enough to see you move into a Quality Relationship or do a runner, at least.

As I said, he may be shocked the frivolous part of the relationship is over and baulk at the thought of labelling the relationship because in a guy's dictionary, 'commitment' is seen to be opposite of homebrew, fishing, wrestling and illegal fireworks night. However, we also know that we can't just go for test-drives mooch around at the dealership forever - eventually we want to buy a car. We're just as nervous about buying a lease as you.

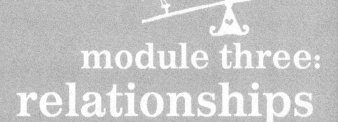

module three:
relationships

1.

Avoid the Boyfriend Cave

In this lesson, you'll learn how to how to avoid accidentally wandering into the Boyfriend Cave, a place where many women find themselves once they start an exclusive relationship, never to re-emerge.

Having said that, there aren't any bats and on Tuesdays we play Scrabble.

Look at you! All happy and exclusive and boyfriendy! *Good for you.* You deserve to feel joyful and smug: you've carefully navigated your way through courting and dating, and you're now wrapped up in the sweet, gentle petals of love with a man who treats you well and makes your insides smile.

Don't let it go to your head.

By all means, dive into this with your eyes closed and a gooey grin etched onto your face, but for the sake of steak sandwiches, *stay on game, girl!* Don't forget who you were before you met this guy. What your life was like a few months back. Your friends. Your jazzercise class. Daily walks. Weekly dinners with mum. That's the stuff that makes you who you are, that's the stuff that attracted Your Boyfriend in

Hang on a minute, you're driving your car into the BC? Fact check: make sure your boyfriend's BC has parking.

the first place, and that's the stuff you do NOT chuck out the car window. Or leave outside the Boyfriend Cave.

DATING DICTIONARY: THE BOYFRIEND CAVE

When you find yourself in a Real Life relationship with a real swell guy, sometimes it can take everything in you not to fall into a world where only You and He exist, and where friends, family, dinners and hobbies fall into a distant second place. Some people call it the Honeymoon Phase, the loved-up stage; I call it the Boyfriend Cave.

I've been there, all my friends have been there and if you haven't been in there yourself, you almost certainly have had a girlfriend who has. Incidentally, one of the defining features of the Cave is that those inside don't usually recognise they're there . . . So maybe you *have* been in there and you just don't know it. (If you see him Friday night, then Saturday afternoon through to Sunday night, chances are you're a Cavewoman.)

Now, this Boyfriend Cave is a plush little den. But girls in there don't usually notice the furnishings because they're too busy staring into the eyes of their Boyfriend, or asking what he's doing later on, or making plans for the two of them, or fighting off the friends knocking at the door asking if they're free at all, for even 30 minutes, this weekend. In fact, the Boyfriend Cave is so comfortable, some women stay in there for so long that it changes into the Husband Cave right before their eyes! Imagine that!

It truly does have the most powerful appeal. I mean,

It's a fairly modern cave, with a door . . . and some arcade machines.

this is a place where all of that hard, time-consuming stuff you do as a Single Girl (maintaining friendships, your card-making business, blogging, saying yes to invitations) fades away, and all you have to think about is what you and Your Boyfriend will do for dinner and which movie you'll see. How awesome! How easy! How perfect for ruining your relationship!

THE PERILS OF BEING A CAVEWOMAN

Giving up your plans, your life and friends to be 100% dedicated to your relationship *sounds* romantic and like it would be just what your lover would want and appreciate . . . but actually works to achieve the direct opposite.

Oh yeah, the Boyfriend Cave is a *real* time sucker. You can be in there for a whole weekend and not even realise it: movie and dinner Friday night, Saturday day trip down the coast, Saturday night pizza and DVDs, Sunday BBQ at his mate's place . . . It's understandable. When you're freshly in love, you can't believe you have got this shiny new person to hang out with, and all the stuff you used to do suddenly starts to look kind of dull in comparison. Especially if you were playing hard ball and keeping up your awesome, busy life during the courting so as to keep him on his toes. It's almost a relief to just go into hiding with your man, isn't it? I mean, finally, you can relax, and just admit how into him you are, and loll around in each other's sensational aura! Right?

Wrong. Wrong as a small curly black hair in your mango gelato. Here's why: leaving your Old Life

you can move around but still be in the cave. It travels on top of you. Like a snail.

Right! No, hang on . . .

behind to immerse yourself fully in a relationship benefits neither you nor your partner.

In doing this, you are:

- placing an enormous amount of pressure on your relationship to provide you with all the excitement, joy and interest that a whole smorgasbord of friendship circles and activities used to fulfil;
- placing an enormous amount of pressure on your partner to make you happy and keep you entertained and busy;
- failing to recognise that the life you enjoyed before was exactly what made you such a catch in his eyes;
- forgetting the sad, unsavoury but inevitable truth that should things ever go sour with your new friend, you will be That Girl – the one who has no friends or life because she ditched them when she met the guy;
- limiting your social circle to one person;
- risking the demise of your new relationship by no longer being able to offer conversations and experiences that differ to your boyfriend's and interest him;
- essentially forgetting who you are and what made you such an interesting, fun creature; and
- inadvertently showing your boyfriend that he is kind of, uh, *your whole world.*

Basically, this is why the 'all-in-one' food pill never took off. You need variety to keep things interesting.

All of this means you have become a bore who only wants to hang out with your boyfriend, and who has forgotten how much more of a person (and partner) you are when you actively maintain your friendships and interests.

I was lucky with one of my boyfriends in that I had no option to do this because he was away so often. Friends would ask if I found it annoying, or if it was hard, and sure, there were moments when I felt like I was a girl in a relationship living a Single Girl's existence, but I soon learned that it actually put me in a terrific position. I was able to enjoy a quality relationship and a quality *life*. My friends could never accuse me of going into the Cave, because I was standing right there next to them, ordering a latte.

And everyone knows there's no espresso machine in the Cave.

I feel very strongly about this whole Cave business. Actually, not so much the Cave, but its opposite: the richness enjoyment of life that comes from having your cake (social, active life) and eating it too (relationship) – and then not having to do any washing up afterwards (happy boyfriend who can't get enough of you because you have your own life and allow him to enjoy his).

There's something very loud and important to be said for having a relationship that is based on *quality* time over *quantity*. When the two of you don't see each other every day, and you both keep your life on a similar frequency to when you were dating, you bring a lot more to the table, both literally (stories from each other's day) and figuratively (your independence, your individual goals and aspirations, your appreciation for each other).

TAKE A TEST

Here's a few hard-hitting questions that will probably make you a little bit defensive and irritable to determine if you're in the Boyfriend Cave.

When was the last time you saw your best friend?
If it was within the last week, great. Last few days? Even better. If it was longer than a week ago, and prior to Being Exclusive with your boyfriend it was daily, you might be in the Boyfriend Cave.

Remember: the saying 'mates before dates' exists for a reason. The passion (and chemical imbalance) that accompanies romantic relationships usually makes them far less reliable than those built on years of friendship. Your best mate deserves a little better than being tossed into the social bin just because you met a dude.

When was the last time you spent a night at home, just being slothy, fake-tanny and face-masky (and not just because He is busy)?
If it was within the last week, excellent. Can't remember? Be careful. When we fall into the pool of love, usually among the first things to go are our rituals and routines . . . that Sunday night home facial, that morning coffee with your gay friend Michael, your Saturday flea market obsession. If you have to stop and think when it was you last did any of these, you might be in the Boyfriend Cave.

When was the last time you slept at your place, alone, because you needed a good sleep?
Can't remember? Hmm. Sleep is a basic human need we often give up when we fall in love. With sleep-overs every night, at his place and our place, we're often not sleeping well (for a plethora of reasons, you kinky little sack monster), but we don't do anything about it because we just want to be with each other

every dingin' second of the day. And night. This comes back to putting your needs first: if you're a walking zombie, and your work, diet and mood are suffering because of your lack of sleep, stop. Tell the boyfriend you're sleeping at home alone tonight. Do it at least once a week. It will regenerate you and it signals to him that you care enough about yourself to look after your body and mind.

Trust me, this will not be met with too much protest. Guys love sleep, perhaps more than girls. Sure, you have Sleeping Beauty, but we have Wee Willie Winkie <u>and</u> Cap'n Snooze.

When was the last time you got up for your early morning walk or went to yoga?
Can't remember? Gone from five days a week to one? Only do it when he goes for a surf? This is definitely Cave material. Like sleep, your health and fitness are also prone to being majorly shafted when you launch into a new relationship. This makes no sense at all: exercise is caring for your body and health, keeps you feeling and looking good, and is superb thinking time (my best book ideas come when I run, which is annoying, because I generally don't run with my laptop). But it's oh so hard to extract yourself from his cosy, warm arms on a cold wintery morning. And it's so easy to meet him straight after work for dinner instead of going to the gym. *Cut it out!* Don't be one of those people who put on weight when they fall in love. It's a billboard saying: I care much more about my relationship than myself. (Which you obviously don't – that'd be nuts.)

When was the last time friends or family made a smartarse quip about how you've gone underground since falling in love?
Yesterday? The last time you saw them? Every time

you see them? Sure, they're joking, but most of the time humour is simply a technique for saying what can't be said without causing offence (e.g. 'Whoa buddy! Is that a mothball I see falling out of your wallet?', meaning, 'You're a cheap son of a bitch and you need to *start paying for rounds*'.)

If your friends are paying you out because they never see you anymore, they're gently whispering into the Cave that they miss you. They mean it with love. It's next to impossible to tell a friend they're engaging in unsafe amounts of boyfriend without causing insult. Take what they say as an objective, well-intentioned alarm bell.

WHAT HAVE YOU LEARNED?

Ever heard of the bends? It's another term for decompression sickness, which scuba divers get when they go too deep or ascend too quickly. The nitrogen in their tanks starts to affect them in the most unsavoury manner: confusion, hallucinations, light-headedness, inability to understand what is reality . . . not great when you're 30 metres underwater and relying on your brain to help you to *not* be 30 metres underwater, and to be, you know, alive and stuff. When you go into the Boyfriend Cave, you have the water-free equivalent of the bends: you're not thinking straight, you forget how you got there, and you don't understand the importance of getting out as soon as possible.

Hopefully now you're aware of the dangers, you'll be able to detect whether you're in the Boyfriend Cave, and if you are, understand that perhaps you need to pull back a little bit and keep in touch with the rest

of your life. By keeping up your social and personal
life, you're strengthening your relationship and giving
it the best chance of longevity.

we don't want to be in the Boyfriend Cave with you either — there
were lots of things outside that we loved doing, like chasing sabre-
toothed tigers, fashioning crude axes better than our friends, and
driving to work in primitive cars where your feet stick out the
bottom. (Some of my research may come from 'The Flintstones'.)
The upshot is, if we can maintain what was important to us in our
old life, and see you doing the same, we will embrace our new
life — and be far less likely to have a panic attack eight years
into the relationship and buy a Harley. Everyone wins (except
the Harley dealer).

2.

Come As You Are: Not Just a Nirvana Song

In this lesson, you'll learn to understand and accept that the one you have entered this relationship with is going to be the one you marry or have children with. (Or else he's the one you're going to leave.)

Hands up if you've ever been in a Quality Relationship, and after, say, seven or eight months of joy, (fun, romance, good sex, great conversation), you find yourself thinking: 'Gosh, things really are going great, but I can't help thinking that if he just got his hair cut . . . or stopped smoking or taking drugs . . . or quit that whole wet-towel-on-the-bed business . . . or started being more affectionate in public . . . *things would be perfect.*'

Then Bang! Kapow! Boom! It hits you. This is your forte, your world! You know what you need to do, because if anyone can make him kick those habits and become a better person – because that will obviously make him a better person in anyone's eye – it's YOU. You are so equipped for this! And you just know he'll be grateful for it in the end. Who wouldn't? I mean, *you* love makeovers, right?

It's no surprise that women like the idea of transforming their mate into the Perfect Man. We do the same with our face every morning, our hair, our bodies, our outfits, our homes . . . we are in a perpetual state of Make Better, if not Make Perfect.

But that doesn't translate to men, or relationships. Here's why.

FIVE SIMPLE TRUTHS: MEN ARE WHAT MEN ARE

Much has been written about the biological, physiological and emotional differences between men and women (amazingly, it's more than just genitalia), and I suggest reading some of it so you don't get upset the next time he doesn't think to leave you some milk for *your* tea.

Till then, here are some home truths about guys, which should assist you in understanding why trying to change them is futile.

1. Men grasp onto their habits and what they know
Take the example of a change in attire or personal appearance. The guy's response to change is: 'Why? I like it this way. It's the way I've always done it.' Whereas the female's argument is: 'But everyone's doing it this way. Looks better this way.' We're more likely to place what we do in a social context. Men, not so much. They don't care – even if we want them to. (This is actually a Good Thing: ask any woman who has dated a metrosexual. Fighting for mirror space or shopping for him for three hours each Saturday is less fun than might be imagined.)

Have you ever seen a dog wearing a novelty outfit, staring at you, wishing it had thumbs so it could get itself out of the sailor suit? Keep that image in your head for this chapter.

I'm surprised there was milk at all.

This is why guys have 15 T-shirts that all look the same.

2. Men think it's if not broke . . .

we would get the toolbox out, but not to fix anything. Just 'cos we like tools.

Don't fix it. Don't even get the toolbox out. Drive straight past Bunnings and do not stop. So long as the relationship is going well – and no one's cheating, no one's fighting and no one's dying – why get hung up on the little things?

3. Men take great pride in knowing more than their girlfriend about things

So when you start asserting that something (like him and his habits and lifestyle) could, in fact, be better, and suggest that he just can't see it, he's likely to become a little bit resistant. Just like when you want him to ask for directions and he refuses. And then you *So, it wasn't* fight. And then you sulk. And then he opens the chips. *all bad.* And you eat some.

4. Who he is defines him

If he turns up to the pub and he's changed from the car guy to the baker, he might get kicked out of the group ('cos we don't really need a baker).

It's taken him years to be known as who he 'is'. That he's the guy who's excellent at darts. The king BBQ-er, or the scholar, or the comedian, or the Ladies Man in his friendship circle. When you come in and try to change him, he feels threatened because it feels as though you are trying to alter the very essence of him. Hence the resistance.

5. Saying he needs changing indicates he's not good enough as is

Surely I don't need to tell you what kind of fat ego blow that is. (Hint: Big. A big one.)

Food for thought: How much do YOU like being told you should be better, or should do things another way?

RECOGNISING THE SIGNS

It might come as you watch or listen while he does something you feel could be improved, or stopped altogether. It might be when he does that slurping thing while he's eating pasta. Or when he hangs out with that dickhead Frank, who has a fetid body odour and an extensive bong collection. It could be when he spends a whole weekend at his dad's place and none at yours. Or when he fails to do that One Thing that would prove he loves you – like saying, 'I love you' at the end of a phone call, or cuddling you throughout the night. Or it could be more big picture. For instance, you might think one day, possibly after a fight: 'I am on the right track in my life – good job, a car, good friends, bought my first apartment – but he is still living with flatmates, in a dead-end job and has no money.'

Suddenly, from the back of your head a honeyed little voice will whisper: 'Hmmm. That could become *really* annoying. Pah. No biggie. I know I can get him to see why he should do things differently.'

Any of this familiar?

1. You think about his deficiencies more than his positive attributes.
2. You seem to be annoyed at him a lot, but he never seems annoyed with you. He claims that you pick all the fights – he just sails along minding his own business until you explode.
3. You find that you're trying not to care about those things you wish he would change (e.g. perving on women all the time, speaking to you in a way that hurts you), but deep down, they continue to perplex you.

4. He's terrible with responsibility, finances, reliability . . .
5. You're frustrated. Often.
6. He's telling you he's 'always been this way', and you still don't believe him.
7. He's not as adoring, loving, caring, romantic, affectionate as you would like him to be, but you tell yourself it will come with time.
8. He's displaying self-destructive or morose behaviour.
9. When you ask if he'll change or moderate his behaviour, he doesn't. (Or he says he will, but his actions indicate otherwise.)

Like a big boat with a tiny rudder, we can make small course adjustments, but we're not about to change which country we're sailing to.

If some of this does sound familiar, it may be time for a re-evaluation of your relationship. He is not going to change. You are not going to change him. Do you love him enough to compromise yourself by accepting his behaviour as is and stay in the relationship? If you do, then whatever it is about him that's causing the problem, you have to let go of it as an issue. If you can't let it go, then let him go. **Because there will be no change.**

He might try to change, and become less messy or more affectionate, or more motivated. Good men want nothing more than for their lady to be happy and will genuinely attempt to be the man you want (just as you try to be the woman he wants). But unfortunately, not even *they* can control this stuff. It's just Who They Are. It's more ingrained than an olive oil stain on a silk dress.

Stop wasting energy on a man you want to change. Instead, find a man you can love for him, *and not the man he* could *be.*

If you can understand this, oh, the peace you will

have! Think of those women – and maybe you've even been one of them – who suffer such violent heartbreak and disillusion when it dawns on them after ten years, when they're married with 2.4 kids: *he's never going to change*. He's always going to be lazy. He's always going to forget to refill the kettle. He's always going to be passive-aggressive. He's always going to walk around nude.

TRYING TO CHANGE HIM ENDS UP CHANGING YOU

Sadly, so many of us fall in love with a man's *potential* rather than the man himself. We then embark on a relationship based on the premise that he is 80% what we want, and we can fix that last 20%. We just know we can make him 'better', or 'rescue' him, or bring out the hidden potential we know is there. (The off-shoot of all this is that when we embark on Project Change, we get to feel good about ourselves for being so caring, tolerant and patient.)

And when we find we can't fix him, we become despondent, resentful and very gnarly indeed. We waste gigatonnes of energy trying to justify his actions when they upset us, in the hope that one day he'll care enough to change those actions. But it's not that he doesn't care. And it's not that he's trying to upset you. It's just how he is.

Hint: Men are not apartments. You can't renovate them. They're heritage-listed.

Don't be angry with him. Accept it and, well, get a grip. For, despite the fact that you're obviously incredibly intelligent, emotionally evolved and good-looking (everyone who bought this book is, by default), there is probably a constellation of things your man would like to change about you. But men tend to be able to accept that that's the way we are . . . Or at least repress their feelings for years, until a huge fight when it all comes tumbling out and you're in shock for several days afterwards. (I've been there, and man is *that* fun.)

I know what you're thinking. I'VE BEEN GYPPED. He was NOT like this when we were dating. And, okay, to an extent, you're right. But honey, you're probably not the same bird fluttering her mascara-laden lashes across a restaurant table, either.

Don't forget that in the early dating days the two of you bonded purely over your likenesses, but unfortunately those heady, halcyon days can't last forever. The dissimilarities always shine through eventually, and not all of them will be pleasant to your partner. You're a cumulative product of nature and nurture, your past relationships and experiences. You have become the way you are over many years. That sort of history is not easily changed. Old dogs, new tricks, etc. And the better grip you have on this, the more likely you're able to avoid this sequence of events:

- he's just getting on with being him;
- you're getting on with trying to change him;
- you're so busy thinking about and/or executing said changes, that you begin to forget who *you* are, and to be grateful for all of the good in the relationship;
- you're not you, and he begins to feel bad about being him; and
- your relationship suffers.

you kind of need to see us as vintage cars – we look okay to the right person, kind of get the job done, and all the bits that are cracked and leak gas 'add adorable character'.

The irony in all this is that when you become fixated on changing things you have no control over, the only one doing any changing is *you*. And not for the good. When you're solely focused on what you don't have, what is wrong and what could be better, you're expending incredible amounts of energy – energy that could surely be better spent on bettering yourself, rather than trying to better your boyfriend.

THE EXCEPTION

If he's destructive, has addictions or constantly dis-respects you, not only should you forget trying to change him, you should probably forget him, full stop. Sometimes he just might not be the right guy for you. And if you believe big changes are needed for him to become right for you, cut your losses and leave. You can't enforce these changes and if he's not making any effort to ramify them, he never will. (If and when he does, it will be because HE chose to, not because his partner wanted him to.)

AFMI (Amazing Final Man Insight):
In essence, think of him like a ball of clay that is actually not clay, but is in fact clay-coloured titanium, and is therefore quite hard to sculpt with your bare hands. You have to love that titanium or leave (which may even be the name of a country music album).

3.

Be a Lover, Not a Mother

In this lesson, you'll learn the importance of keeping your Sexy Jeans on and your Mum Jeans folded up neatly in the back of the cupboard.

There's a lot written about how many men end up with women who resemble their mother in some way (provided she wasn't a junkie with a string of mob boyfriends). As their son's first, and usually biggest, influence, their mothers become a kind of subconscious role model for womanhood. What this means for you is that if his mum is an exceptional cook, guess what he'll come to expect from you. If his mum was a hard-working career woman, he might not be *that* thrilled with your desire to become a stay-at-home mum.

On the other hand, there are the guys who go for the complete opposite.* Be mindful that these guys are usually highly sensitive to anything their girlfriends do that even remotely smells like something their mother might do. It's kind of like you baulking at a guy who gets his aggression on at the drop of a hat, just like your dad did, and it brings back unsavoury memories.

*without going as far as dating their dad.

Whether either of these is true of your guy, your job is not to compare yourself to his mother. And your job is absolutely, 100% to avoid *acting* like his mother, your mother, or anyone's mother. Good or bad. Sweet or cynical. Adoring or berating. For some peculiar reason a lot of women are independent, sexy, cool, flexible and fun while dating or courting, but once they're settled in relationship, they morph into some kind of nagging, lecturing mother type. Don't do it.

Disclaimer: For the purposes of this lesson, a 'mother' isn't the cool kind that lets you stay up and drink beers with your friends. She's more the nagging, overbearing, overly mummying breed. The type who continually dishes out negative reminders about what her boy has done and how he should have done it, or what he hasn't done. The type who knows exactly the end result of every situation before it happens. (And mum, if you're reading this, this is SO not you. You're awesome.)

THE NAGGING MOTHER

Your role in a relationship is not to be the angry, nagging girl who reminds their boyfriend of a past naggy, whiny girlfriend, or his best mate's ball-breaking girlfriend, or his mother. Criticising, or advising him lovingly how he could do things better, or look better or behave better, contrary to what you might think, does *not* demonstrate how much you care for him. It demonstrates that you're a pain in the arse. I know this, because I'm as guilty of this behaviour as the Hamburgler is of stealing cheeseburgers.

• Yes, he *will* be hung-over tomorrow if he stays

As a rite of passage, once any guy pays his first rent cheque as a young man, it is subconsciously understood he should never hear these phrases again, or something is wrong.

out and drinks till 4 a.m. He knows this. You don't need to remind him.

- Yes, his hair looks better when it's cut short and when he grows his beard a touch. He knows this. You don't need to remind him.
- Yes, his brother is a jackass who always borrows money off him and never pays it back. He knows this. You don't need to remind him.
- Yes, he needs to renew his gym membership. He knows this. You don't need to remind him.

Yes, you're honestly trying to help when you raise these things. Don't worry, I get it. You're a gem. I see that.

Unfortunately, all *he* hears is: 'HEY! Listen to me! I have information about your life that you're not intelligent enough to figure out for yourself.' In other words, you kind of sound like his mother.

Try to imagine if he did this to you, telling you not to drive if you've been drinking, warning you that that friend is not worth hanging out with, educating you on the perils of not buying tickets for that show until the week it's on. In all likelihood, you'd want to prick your eyeballs with small pins. And that's how he feels when you do it to him. So **cut it out.** It's not cute, it's not sexy, and it's probably not even you. We usually become like this out of some deep-seated need to control him, of needing to assume some kind of power over his life.

Well, why else would you be doing it? You've invested in this man, now you want to be sure he is as dedicated to The Cause as you are. And how to do this? By ensuring you have some kind of authority over every little aspect of his life. Who he's on the phone to. Who he goes out with. What time he'll be coming over. Man, even writing this stuff is making me squirm.

Example: The Lover or the Mother?

The lover gets annoyed about the fact that he rocks up 25 minutes late for a date and expresses this by saying: 'I'm a bit pissed off, actually. Don't do that again, or at the very least give me a heads up.'

The guy says, 'Sorry babe. Good call.'

The mother says, 'Surprise, surprise, you're late. I busted my arse getting ready on time after work to be here for 7 and you just rock up when it suits you. It's like you don't even think of me, just yourself.'

The guy says: 'I didn't ask to be born! Anthony's parents let him do whatever he wants! I HATE you!'

He doesn't love you any less when you **don't** *comment on his behaviour, but he will start to love you less when you do.*

THE FUSSING MOTHER

The other mothering best avoided is waiting on him hand and foot. Because despite what men think they want (a woman who does everything for them), they actually don't want this at all. I mean, sure, most men love it superficially – who wouldn't love home-cooked meals and a fully stocked fridge? – but a woman who always puts her boyfriend's needs before hers (sometimes to the point of martyrdom), does not make for a happy relationship.

which we all figured out back when smoking was thought to cleanse the lungs.

And all this correcting and directing and reminding and berating? It comes from an unhealthy place – we're treating men as though they're incompetent in order to prove that we're indispensible. We're showing how amazing and nurturing we are, almost in expectation of being rewarded for it, but instead he just ends up feeling like a child (cue rebellion and resentment).

CASE STUDY

Lily and Isaac have been dating for 18 months. They have been very happy, Isaac especially. Lily is Top Shelf, the kind of girl who loves to cook, can't resist cleaning up just a little when she stays over, and always picks him up from the airport, even if his flight gets in at 5.55 a.m. She plays designated driver without batting an eyelid and always ensures he and his mates are well looked after on mornings following a Big One.

Marry me, Lily. (Sorry, Isaac.)

Lily is starting to feel a little bit confused. She feels she's been doing all the right things, being the Perfect Girlfriend (PG), but apparently it isn't inspiring Isaac to move the relationship forward in any way. She thought that by showing him what a domestic goddess she was, and how caring, considerate and cool she was, he would see the benefits of her moving in and, well, maybe even a marriage proposal. But it hasn't happened.

The relationship could now go several ways – here are a few of the more common scenarios. Which do you think is best?

Scenario one

After a few more months of sticking to her PG rating, Lily asks Isaac for 'a talk' and tells him that she thinks they should be taking the relationship to the 'next level'. Isaac is baffled. He doesn't understand where this all came from! He thinks things are great just the way they are. He certainly isn't ready to live with Lily, as delightful as she is. He's too young! He'd feel cramped. So he tells her he's not ready just yet, that things are going so well, they should just play it out it till Christmas and then see how things are after they go on their trip to Thailand. Lily feels disappointed, but figures she's on the right path at least. And he did say they would talk about it after Thailand. He's right, what's the rush, she thinks, as she goes to get his clothes out of the dryer.

If that really worked, he should try selling her some Lunar Real Estate.

Scenario two

Midway through cooking Isaac's favourite lamb roast, Lily has a light-bulb moment. She looks over to where he's sitting watching the news and a flash of rage rips through her. This is not her apartment, yet she cooks and cleans and stays in it as though it were. Isaac won't even get off his arse to make a salad even though she has now asked three times, and SHE DOESN'T EVEN LIKE LAMB. She realises she's become his servile mother. She's lost her sexy girlfriend vibe. She's created a relationship tailored entirely to his needs and yet he is utterly unappreciative. *He will probably never even ask her to move in!* Fuck this, enough is enough. She decides to show him just how much she does for him, by pulling it out from under his feet. After dinner, she doesn't clean up, she goes home and plans a *big* weekend with her best girlfriends. Lily keeps up this new regime for a few weeks. The change in Isaac is immeasurable: suddenly he needs to fight for her time, which makes him more affectionate and appreciative of the time he has with her, and he's far randier than he's been in a long time. Lily is thrilled with the results of her experiment: she's become his *lover* again and both of them are benefiting enormously.

Despite what Britney said, being a 'Slave 4 U' eventually will stop working for us. And not just because it looks like a six-year-old spelled it.

Scenario three

Cut to a few months later and Isaac has realised he has feelings for a girl in his office, Maude. She's dynamic and exciting, and all the guys are after her. Issac and Maude email a lot, and at after-work drinks he finds himself wanting very much to stay and drink all night with her, rather than go home to Lily. Oh, he loves Lily – very much – but he just finds her a little, well, *Lily*. She doesn't keep him on his toes like Maude does. Lily's so loving and sweet . . . but so predictable. If only he could put her on ice till he wants to settle down. More and more, he snaps at Lily. She does something kind or cute and it only irritates him. Lily's left very upset. She thinks she's doing everything right and he's being an arsehole. Eventually, after a drunken night out, the inevitable occurs: Isaac hooks up with Maude. And then it happens again. And again. Eventually, Lily can't handle Isaac's moods and attitude anymore (which is kind of Isaac's plan – to make Lily do the dumping so he doesn't have to deal with it), and she breaks up with him, never understanding what went wrong and completely unsure how to conduct herself in relationships. She thought that by playing Perfect Girlfriend she would secure a loving man and happy relationship, but she was brutally deprived of both.

How did you go?

The winning scenario is clearly the one where Lily realises she is working towards the wrong goal. **That in trying to create an environment that breeds commitment, she is in fact preventing it.** When Lily began behaving in a way that was true to herself, and stopped caring so much about what Isaac wanted, what he was doing and whether he was happy, he immediately began responding in a favourable fashion.

Despite what men think, or want, or expect, or even aspire to, they really don't want someone fussing over them. They don't want someone living half a life so that they may have a perfect one, or someone constantly observing and analysing what they're doing or have done. They want the girl who cares, but cares enough not to remove the fire and attraction from the relationship.

It's not sexy to be waited on hand and foot — eventually it'll make us feel 17 again and we'll want to 'move out'. To another girl's house. Ouch.

HANDY HINT

Treat your boyfriend as you do your friend. Would you bitch out a friend for letting their boss belittle them in a meeting? Would you tell them those shoes looked super wrongo with those jeans? Pick flaws in their family? Get pissed at them for needing to push the Friday night movie to Saturday night? No. (And if you did, you probably wouldn't have many friends and they'd all bitch about you when you're not there.)

I don't peer at a friend suspiciously if he tells me he's going to take a trip to Mexico with some friends. I don't suggest to a workmate that her conduct in that business meeting was rubbish. But with boyfriends, it just seems to fall from my mouth. *I* know what is best for him, about everything, always. If he does something that I feel could have been done better, I tell him. Usually without even thinking about what a little snot I'm being. And let me tell you, if my boyfriend

---

behaved like this with me? Telling me what was best for me, reigning me in when I was doing something that didn't fit his mould of who I should be? I would *not* be sticking around. Laterz, amigo.

For some reason, boyfriends can miss out on the leeway, and politeness and pleasantries, usually granted to friends, and instead can get thumped with criticism. But they SHOULDN'T. In fact, we should be treating them up there with the best. *We love them*, remember?*

*'Cos they're super-great guys who you should give lots of massages to. (I'll admit to occasionally abusing my role in this book in the hope my girlfriend reads it).

WHAT HAVE YOU LEARNED?

Keep in mind that this is all stuff you've got to do from the outset. The architecture of this book is chronological for a reason. The first two modules were designed to establish things like self-love, confidence, positive selfishness, a high Perceived Value, and knowledge of how to control the pace of the relationship, so that when you got into mid- to long-term dating with a guy, you were a formidable dating machine. So now you love yourself, you love him, he loves and appreciates you. What a dream.

But then life happens. And old habits or new fears sometimes slip in for a coffee and a ciggy and cause some commotion. And this goes for all the different girlfriend types out there, from the easygoing flowers to the demanding fascists – we're all susceptible of behaviour that sabotages our relationship.

But if one day you notice that he's not responding to you as he used to, and you attempt to suddenly click back into the hardcore, super-foxy Beyoncé woman that he fell in love with, well, it's a little like closing the barn door after the bull has bolted.

The key – and this is a Big Key – is being consistently independent and challenging for him. And this is not game-playing – this needs to be something that is ingrained in you. Why do you *really* care what time he gets home? Or if he's hung-over all day Sunday? Provided neither affects you or plans you had in place, so what? Or if his gym membership expires? So what? That's his problem! Who cares? Is it going to ruin your weekend? Your week? Your life? Your relationship? No, it's not. Let him be, and more often than not, he will choose to be with you. Be his lover, be the fun, interesting woman with him that you are with everyone else, and watch how the dynamic of your relationship shifts.

Or walked off in despair – either way, you're down a bull.

Guys are not complicated beings. They're happy doing what they're doing (unless you see them in a haberdashery store, but I guarantee they're not in there voluntarily) and they want you to be a part of it, not restrict it. This doesn't mean we should get away with whatever we want (i.e. we claim it's acceptable to have a stripper over because 'it's a Saturday, or Tuesday or Thursday'), but for the small stuff, you don't want to feel you have to be scared of getting in trouble. Once a guy feels you're being his mum, it's hard to shake the thought. Eventually he'll end up getting heaps of dirty magazines and hiding them under the bed, and stealing money from your wallet for ice-creams.

4.

Would You Rather Be Right, Or Happy?

In this lesson, you'll be reminded of the art of balancing your nurturing and tough energies, and the power of making your man feel like, well, a man.

I feel it's worth reminding you that within all of these hardcore lessons, rules, regulations and drastic alterations to how you've been doing things for many years, sometimes it's easy to lose, or at least play down, your soft, loving, nurturing side. But we don't want that! It's a balance. I just bang on more about the hard-arse stuff because that tends to be the stuff women find harder to do and easier to chuck in.

Like connecting Foxtel to a DVD recorder.

DATING DICTIONARY: EGO MASSAGING

The male ego is not to be underestimated. Ever. And the sooner you realise this, the sooner you two can get on with being all happy and loved up and shit.

While men will rarely admit it, they all need to be

made to feel manly.* Even the ones who wear a daisy chain and no shoes, and carry around a small banjo. (We're still in 1971, right?) There is a simple way to cater to this. Learn the art of Ego Massaging and use it freely. If you do it for long enough, it will become second nature.

For simplicity, let's compartmentalise his ego into **The Provider**, **The Lover** and **The Thinker**.

The Provider needs to feel like he is able to offer you something, even if you earn your own cash (*especially* if you earn more than him), and have your own car, pad etc., and don't actually 'need' him. Let him know you appreciate all of his efforts and that they make a difference. Always show your gratitude whenever he pays or buys you something. Sometimes it's worth creating a situation where you can allow him to be The Provider, such as asking him to help you hang a painting, or set up the DVD player, or check the tyre pressure in your Aston Martin. Yes, I realise how drastically warped and *Stepford Wives* this sounds. Don't care. It works.

The Lover needs to know he looks hot in that grey v-neck T-shirt, he's a right sight with his shirt off and he's amazing in the bedroom. If he has a beer gut, focus on his hair. If he's bald, focus on his smile. Whatever it is, just remember how important it is to talk up your man's physicality, sexual prowess and appearance. You love it when he does it for you – so pay it forward and watch him shine in your glowing admiration.

The Thinker needs to know he is clever, talented and of value. This is a time for you to be specific and

*Hence the existence of woodchopping competitions.

Like when he brings you a dead mouse and lays it on the back door ... not actually too different.

If you sell it convincingly enough, we even fall for, 'I love the end of your nose, it's so cute'. I'm not joking. I'm still holding onto that compliment.

harness the power of the Third Party Compliment. An example: he pulled off a coup at work. You congratulate him privately, but the next time you're with other people, say, at a dinner party, make a reasonable-sized deal about how well he's going at work (not too much or it could be embarrassing). He'll play it down, but it's your job to get in there and talk him up so that everyone sees how much you think of him and his astonishing business acumen. Bang. Double point score. Another way to do this is when you're on the phone and he's in earshot. Talk up the fact he came and picked you up from work, or fixed the bathroom light, or cooked you lobster mornay. Simple, but effective.

I realise that what I am asking you to do may seem contrived and kind of retarded. I do. But it's **not**. Having the grace and self-confidence to compliment your partner, to verbalise your appreciation, is a beautiful thing. The trouble is, we modern, independent young things sometimes find it hard to pour the praise onto our partners, because it feels somehow insincere, or like we're 'letting them win' in some way. But is it insincere when you tell your best friend she is AMAZ-ING in 13 texts, two phone calls and a card after she wins that National Karaoke Competition? Or when you email your brother telling him how proud of him you are for getting that promotion? No. Give with love and not resentment or pride. Give because you love this guy and it won't kill you to flatter his ego a little now and then. After all – how much do you love it when he talks *you* up? Lots.

Sometimes I watch the happiest couple I know (my

It really isn't contrived. Basically our ego is like a small puppy who bloody loves a good tummy scratch.

Relationship Idols – we all need to have them, just as you have a career mentor), who have been married for 35 plus years, and so much of their interaction is talking each other up and showing pride in each other's abilities and talents. Even things like how she serves his dinner. How he reverse parks. And the best part is, it's *genuine*. They truly do believe their partner is fabulous at a LOT of things, and they love to tell them so. There is a constant flow of admiration and gratitude, and *man*, is it a solid foundation for a truly beautiful relationship.

Support him when he's at his lowest, and support him when he's punching the air and performing sailor-esque ankle-clicks with joy. Projecting appreciation and admiration has an extremely powerful effect – if you're in a healthy, abundant, loving frame of mind you attract what you are putting out. Cue willing-to-please, loving partner and mutually adoring relationship. (And then the dancing monkeys.)

Guy Fact: we remember compliments when we're hurting more than when we're flying. we don't forget, either – like when you tell an elephant it has excellent tusks.

HARNESS THE POWER OF YIN AND YANG

My girlfriends and I agree that one of the hardest things women have to learn is the art of juggling being the assertive, alpha female at work all day, and then coming home and clicking into the sweet, gentle pussycat who cooks dinner and asks how her man's day was as she fetches his pipe and slippers. (That might be an exaggeration, thieved from a '60s TV show and/or entirely untrue.)

Having different roles in different areas of your life is to be expected, but shutting off the part of you that creates and enforces order for nine hours of the day, whether in the workplace or with your children, to become a compliant, pleasant dinner partner is not always possible.

This is a myth. You don't need to become the pipe-fetcher once you meet up with your boyfriend. You don't *need* to assume the subservient, sweet role. But you do need to remember that in a relationship, there's always that Yin and Yang energy transaction.

One person must display the softer, feminine characteristics of Yin and one the strength and masculinity of Yang. Otherwise there'll be a clashing of energy (technical term: fights).

Yin and Yang are a kismet pair; one cannot exist without the other. If you sense the presence of Yin, you will probably unconsciously start to channel some Yang. (If, for example, your boyfriend is being indecisive about where to go for dinner and deferring to what you want to do, you need to step in and take control.) Similarly, if you detect Yang, well, that's when you need to pop your Yin cap on.* (He has decided on the dinner venue and what time he'll pick you up.)

*Hint: There aren't actually caps – I asked. you're just meant to feel it.

It's helpful to remember the ability to shift energy when:

- You've been channelling Yang energy all day, and then find yourself at dinner with someone who has already bagsed the Yang energy. Soften up, let him lead. You can't *both* dominate.
- He's *very* hungry and shirty, and even if he usually plays the role of cool, easygoing Yin guy, he has switched over to Yang. Move into Yin and allow his Yanginess.
- You're both feeling Yang. Don't wait for him

to shuffle into Yin, you just get on in there and make things pleasant.

A simple way to remember all of this – like, *really* simple (as in, possibly offensive to the whole premise of this Eastern philosophy) – is: **Never both be angry at the same time.** Learn how to move and flow with your partner's energy. Some of the strongest, happiest couples earn those adjectives just by remembering this one rule.

FIGHT FAIR

I once had an editor who told me in one of my more flarey-nostrilled moments – about Editorial Integrity vs Those Mongrels in Advertising – that you should always choose your battles wisely. Lose the battle but win the war, she said. I find it to be an especially salient slice of advice when it comes to arguments with your boyfriend. My mum's line was always, 'Will this matter in an hour? In a day? In a week?' Usually the answer is no. (If the answer is yes, because he went to a strip club when you specifically forbade him to, it's your own fault for not fitting him with a GPS chip.)

Perhaps we'll alter the wording a little to make it: 'Win the man, not the argument'. Would you rather be right or be happy? Exactly.

Other Helpful Anti-Fight Techniques
• Never bring up old incidents – one barney at a time, please.
• Never raise your voice.
• If one of you is going APESHIT, the other one

No bats, no chains, only medium-strength mace.

has to become super-Yin to keep things balanced.
- Never attack or make it personal – you can never get those words back.
- Remember that a lot of the time, it's your ego that wants to win the argument for the sake of winning, rather than your attachment to your standpoint about the fact that you *definitely* turn left, not right at the Myrtle Street exit to get to Dave and Belinda's place.
- If you sense your Reptile Brain is starting to emerge, *stop*, let him talk and slowly count to ten in your head (. . . *then* throw the sucker punch).
- If it's seriously escalating, leave the room. Not in a door-slammy way, but in an adult, 'I think I need to take five' way.
- If there's something upsetting you about the relationship but you haven't sorted it out properly in your head, don't suddenly bring it up in a fight simply because your angry neurons are firing.
- Don't drink and argue.
- Avoid using any 'surprise' ammunition, such as the fact you're actually pregnant, or in therapy, or having a sex change.
- Don't use fights as an excuse to unleash all the things you've been pissed about for the last few months. Wrong time, wrong execution.

Provide salted nuts – this will calm him (or kill him if he has high cholesterol).

It's simple. Discuss things one at a time. Keep an open mind and don't talk over one another. The finest trick you'll ever learn from a psychologist is to shut up and listen. Try it. Not only will it save you from going off your nut and spewing up anger and accusations, you'll leave the floor for him to talk – and sometimes that kind of non-interrupted communication is all that's needed for resolution.

DON'T PUSH WHEN HE PULLS

Occasionally, we feel like the men we love pull away, no matter how faintly, and this is generally not a great feeling. We feel offended or hurt, when in fact what they're doing is completely normal and nothing to lose your shit over.

When you've enjoyed him chasing and adoring you for the entire relationship and he suddenly retreats, it's easy to start thinking it's the first hint that he's unhappy. But usually it's nothing of the kind. It's just Man Time. Sometimes it comes in the shape of extended visits to the pub or golf course, a surfing trip or maybe just sitting at their mate's place drinking beer and Skyping their mate Jimmy in London. But there is no need at all for you to start clambering after him to question why he's doing it, or what it means.

You see, things generally move back at the same rate that we push towards them. And when we pull back, we experience that same rate of push towards us. So, instead of probing him what's wrong, or wondering if he's falling out of love with you, stay put. Get busy, stop analysing it and master the art of overriding the natural push forward you feel when your partner pulls back. If you can do this, you're placing yourself in a very positive position because, in the bigger scheme of things, the ability to take a deep breath and pull back from a situation that is frustrating or confusing permits you to gracefully move forward.

When I was in my very early twenties, I was

atrocious at playing cool in this situation. The nano-second a boyfriend started amping up his Man Time, or going out more often, I panicked. I would watch my phone like a hawk, waiting for him to call. I'd assume the absolute worst when I called and he didn't answer. And the more I let paranoia, fear and overanalysis rule my head, instead of being calm and rational, the further I pushed him away.

Taking a step back in these situations, rather than racing in, will place you in an infinitely better position. You'll get clarity. You'll get perspective. You'll learn the powerful art of composure. Taking some time out and removing yourself from things for a little (physically, mentally and emotionally) while is the best, fastest and more empowered way to heal things. It gives you the space and time to achieve lucidity, but more importantly, it allows him to get the space he was craving (and remember, *very* few men will actually verbalise this need for solo or mate time, they'll just start doing it more). He'll be grateful, and love you even more for allowing him to go about Man Time in peace.

It's why in police movies they always pull the renegade detective off the case, 'cos he's too 'emotionally involved'.

It's not an assault on your relationship. Let him be and, more often than not, he'll be back before you know it. Chase him and question him, on the other hand, and there's a good chance he'll do the very thing you feared he was doing in the first place.

KINDNESS IS NOT EQUAL TO WEAKNESS

Often we get confused about the role of kindness in relationships. But, there is never an excuse for not being kind, caring and loving – in any aspect of your life. As women, these qualities define us. We're called the fairer sex not because we cheat less at Uno, but because we have an innate desire to care about the welfare of others.

I am *violently* aware that this softness and vulnerability seems to conflict with all the Hardcore Bitch stuff you have learned in the lessons preceding this one. I know it as a person who has struggled with this exact conflict in Real Life. But not only can the two co-exist, they **must**. The key is to understand that being caring, gentle and thoughtful towards your boyfriend is not in any way a sign of weakness. It's a sign of being balanced, of loving yourself enough not to worry about pride or getting hurt by appearing to be too soft.

It's not a case of having done all of this hard work to get him to fall for your alluring independence and assertiveness, and develop a long-term relationship with you, only for you to now pull out that old, it's-all-about-him mindset. Uh-uh. There is a stratospheric difference between a doormat and being of kind heart. As emotionally evolved women, we must maintain beautiful traits like kind-heartedness, thoughtfulness, benevolence and empathy in our relationships, and, in fact, in all aspects of life. It's part of what makes us so splendid.*

*Side cleavage ... No?

Say he's had a shit day. You both knew it would be rough in advance, and it was.

Too much: Text all day to check how he is, buy him a little gift, make an enormous deal of a meal, ask him to tell you everything, and follow up the day after with a note of encouragement under his windscreen wiper.

Just right: Come over to his place, pour him a glass of red, ask if he wants to talk about it and take care of dinner.

Not enough: Text (not call) to see if he's okay and, because he says he's fine, keep your plans to check out that new wine bar with Mandy.

TMNT (Tiny Man Nugget of Thought):
This is a really important lesson. If we wanted someone with sexy curled hair to be cold to us just when we needed support, we'd just get Jase to put a wig on. We men don't open up to each other that much. If we open up to you, and you're kind and beautiful, we remember that level of customer service and next time we need someone to get our party supplies, we'll highly recommend you. (Sorry, halfway through that it became a testimonial for Pete's Party Palace, but the theory is the same.)

5.

Don't Move In Till You Get the Ring

In this lesson, you'll get the most important advice you'll ever learn (save for that one about holding your breath underwater): keep your relationship romantic, not domestic.

(**Please note:** This entire chapter revolves around the assumption that you hope to get married. Of course, plenty of people don't bother with weddings these days, so feel free to skip this chapter, or substitute 'kids' for 'marriage', or just become grossly offended that a book published in the 21st century teaches women how to drag an engagement ring out of men.)

There are yillions (that's a number, right?) of confused, hopeful young women out there who are in a long-term relationship with a guy they love very much, but are exasperated that things won't advance to the Next Level.

Women become focused on the Next Level when they decide their guy should definitely be Their Husband/Father of Their Children because he is absolutely terrific, being with any other man is simply unthinkable

It's just after nine dillion.

I would use a video game analogy here about 'Next Levels', but I realise you're almost definitely a girl if you're reading this.

and marriage is a splendid way to cement the love and respect you have for each other.

Unfortunately, in this situation we women are in a bit of a bind. We're not meant to push things along or passive-aggressively point out all of our engaged friends with a wistful look in our eyes. We're certainly not meant to raise the topic of marriage, or drop hints about engagement rings, or show excessive cluckiness around our sister's kids. We're meant to sit back and wait for him to suddenly decide he wants to make us his wife.

Understandably, this kind of passive stance is enough to inspire acute frustration, especially when you're dealing with women who are absolutely in control in every other aspect of their lives. I've sat with many a girlfriend and raged about how, despite the fact that WE are the ones who have to have the children, and WE are the ones who have to put our career on hold, and WE are the ones who end up planning the wedding, we have *absolutely no say* in *when* any of it happens. We just have to sit there, whittling small wooden boats and knitting woollen underpants until HE decides the time is right. The sheer *inactivity* of it all is discombobulating! Exasperating! I mean, we're *modern women!* We buy our own houses! Earn our own cash! Own our own companies!

But here's the thing. Actually, here are five things.

FIVE REASONS NOT TO PUSH THE MARRIAGE THING

1. Just as he has to chase and seduce you into a relationship, he needs to feel like he *wooed you*

into marrying him. This is crucial for the long-term happiness of your relationship: men like to feel as though they won you over; women like to feel as though they are a prize.

2. Hints do not work on men.* Unless they are overt, in which case they become annoying and then infuriating.

3. Men need to feel like marriage was their idea. If it feels like it was your idea, he thinks he was somehow coerced into it, which is a breeding ground for that most dangerous, furious relationship killer – resentment.

4. If you have to encourage him to think he should marry you, maybe you need to consider why he's not already thinking of it, or hasn't already done it. Just sayin'.

5. There could be an entirely legitimate reason as to why he has not proposed yet.

Is that making sense? I hope so. Because this is kind of a big one. Do NOT drop the ball now. (I promise you there will be more than just cut oranges if you play it right.)

Even in pantomimes. How many times must you shout, 'He's behind you!' before the wizard realises that the dragon is, in fact, behind him?

There will be cut-up diamonds. Although I know several thrifty guys who would prefer to give an engagement orange.

THE RIGHT AND WRONG PATHS TO COMMITMENT

Keeping things romantic, not domestic = A much faster, happier path to commitment, and a longer, more satisfying relationship.

Sometimes people learn more from lessons when they are shown the **wrong** way to go about things. Let's find out if you are one of them.

Bear in mind these moves are as subtle as a sledgehammer to the cynical male brain.

What <u>not</u> to do if you want commitment

- Start leaving more stuff at his place as a clue as to how things 'could be'.
- Stop dressing up for him or making an effort with your appearance.
- Drop hints about getting married.
- Compare your relationship to everyone else's (oh, do guys love this one).
- Start considering a hot date to be one in which you turn the heater on while watching a DVD.
- Start spending *more* time with your man, in the ridiculous hope that this will make him want to spend *more* time with you.
- Talk constantly with your girlfriends about how much you want to get engaged and how annoyed you are with his lack of activity.

• Anything that involves handcuffs in a non-sexual context.

- Assume every holiday or special occasion is *totally* going to be Ring Time.
- Insist that you two should move in together, or excessively hint at it.

What to do if you want commitment

- Keep on enjoying your life just the way it is.
- Keep out of the Boyfriend Cave, and remain active and social, making the most of every day and weekend.
- Be grateful for all that you have, including the great man who loves you, and the great relationship you have with him.
- Withdraw a little from your usual, perhaps stale activities with your boyfriend. Do you *really* need to go to his family dinner each Monday night?

- Remember that good things really do come to those who wait.
- Stop seeing living together as the Holy Grail. It's madness to think that by living with him, being around him every day and night, he'll suddenly be inspired to drop a fat diamond into your lap.
- Stop dropping hints. If he's planning on proposing, each time you hint about it you're adding another six months to when he's going to do it. *No guy* wants to feel like his special grand romantic gesture is expected.
- Remember the Golden, no, PLATINUM Rule: men respond not to what they have, but to what they don't have. If you're around him all the time, he will not act.

REGARDING LIVING WITH HIM

Living with a man can be a wonderful thing. A lot of girls I know adore having their man around sharing breakfast over the Sunday papers, snuggling at night, doing the cooking and grocery shopping together, and sharing one sink as they floss at night. Good for them! Some of these women genuinely don't give a rats about marriage, and don't feel the need to look past the fact that they're living with the man they love. This is a magnificent, mature, modern sentiment and should be commended.

Others think that it's *preposterous* to assume a man would ever consider popping a rock on the third-left without having lived with his missus first. After all, you have to see if you're compatible. If you can live together as adults. If you still love him after discovering he is the leader of the United Front for the Distribution of Dirty Underpants.

But the original thesis behind engagement was for toe dipping. *Engagement* was a trial. So, I pose the question: why the need for a trial period before the trial period? What do you think will change between living together and living together with a princess-cut diamond?

It should be noted here that I once went against my own advice and moved in with a long-term boyfriend. (Well, you can't very well write a book about not doing something if you've never tried it, can you? That would be like writing a book on having a brutal heroin addiction having never had anything harder than chamomile tea.) This gave me a chance to see the positives and negatives of living together before having a solid commitment in place. And while I had a great time playing house, I still believe that if your goal is marriage, and the pursuit of romantic longevity, there is something (quite loud) to be said for holding off on cohabitation until he has expressed an explicit desire to marry you.

Although one might say, 'How do you know you don't like living with tigers until you've lived in a tiger's cage?'

Here's why. If your main, overriding objective is to propel things towards rings and dress fittings, moving in with him is the equivalent of injecting a horse tranquiliser into your relationship. You mistakenly believe it will speed things up. That it will enthuse his willingness to settle down. That it will make him see what a sterling wifey figure you make, because *look!* You're cooking and cleaning, and you're flexible and cool and don't nag about the fact he dumps his shoes at the door and you always trip over them, or that he never walks or feeds Señor Woof. In short, you're heaven, the perfect marriage material.

But, in fact, moving in can slow things down to roughly the rate of soybean growth.

Think about it. You were your best self, and at your most attractive to him when you were an interesting, busy, sexy single woman. When the two of you Became Exclusive, even if you slept together six nights a week, you still lived in different houses and each still had that one glorious night a week to fake tan/call your sister/watch *CSI* (you) or drink beer/fart/watch porn (him).

That one night apart makes an enormous difference to the dynamic of a relationship. (And it's priceless, so the fact you're paying a lot of rent for not much sleeping at home is not a valid argument. Sorry.) It brings with it positive selfishness, freedom and privacy and revitalises the spirit. It reminds you that you're individuals, not just one half of a couple. And at this stage of your relationship, when you're still mortgage-/dog-/children-free, you're doing yourself and your relationship a great service by making the most of this time not living together.

Strangely, drunk, nude girls farting isn't as good as those three things separately.

VISUALISATION EXERCISE

Pretend you are A Boyfriend. Which girlfriend would you probably be more inspired to propose to, assuming you have been with her for two years, you love her very much, and you're ready to do the whole settling-down thing?

A. The girl who you see naked every night and morning, who clips her toenails in front of you, who leaves her Bonds on the bathroom floor, who stays up late watching *Boston Legal* when you're trying to sleep, and who knows exactly what time you got home this morning (6.12 a.m.) and hammers you about it for the next three days.

B. The girl who lives with her flatmate two suburbs away, who stays over a few nights a week but who does her own thing at least two nights a week (making for interesting conversation and far more of a thrill when you get to see her starkers), who you get to see with a Finished Look when you arrive at her place/work to pick her up for dinner, who you never hear swearing about the neighbour's barking dog or wearing those scary face masks that look like Jason from the *Friday the 13th* movies.

C. The girl with the crazy-rich dad who looks like Heidi Klum.

I'm not going to bang on about the correct answer, because you already know that C was a joke (girls like that tend to go for rock stars, whereas you're just a girl reading a book pretending to be a guy) – B is the clear winner. And you know why. See my point, a point good enough to have an increased font size?

Keep things romantic rather than domestic.

I am *such* a devoted subscriber to this mindset. Maybe because I've seen my parents do it with such blinding success. (They stopped sleeping in the same bed when I was a teenager because of Dad's getting up early to write, and now they pretty much live in different houses, choosing to have romantic 'Date Weekends' instead of being in each other's face every day and night. I would be the same after raising eight kids, I imagine.) And guess what: they're still attracted to each other, still romantic and still interested in each other's lives, even after 30-plus years of marriage.

It comes down to enjoying quality time with your boyfriend, as opposed to quantity. About re-grouping with excitement and interesting tales about your life to share, about maintaining that tiny bit of mystery – even if it's only one night a week's worth – just like when you were first dating.

Just think for a moment how much more you appreciate seeing your boyfriend, and how much more sparky the time spent together is, when you haven't seen him for a few days, as opposed to seeing him every day. Routine kills romance and a solid relationship depends on quality time, not quantity. Tattoo that onto your wrist like a good girl, and never forget it.

There is something to be said for looking at your lives together as a book, and deciding how much of the ending you want to show him before he decides to commit to buying (for the price of one diamond ring, thanks).

THE POWER OF DEPRIVATION

Why would any man feel compelled to pop the proverbial if he's already getting a live-in lover, cook and bathroom towel picker-up-er-er? If you're already living together, he has no impetus to upgrade things. It's that whole why-buy-the-sheep-if-you're-already-getting-the-eggs-for-free thing. If you're already living together, it's going to take him a whole lot longer (if at all) to move things to the Next Level because he *isn't being deprived of anything.* I've seen this happen time and time again: girl moves in, delighted and excited, thinking that because her boyfriend's happy to do *that,* the next diamond-encrusted step must be just around the corner. Fast-forward three years and she's still waiting.

It's human nature that we usually only respond when we're in a state of depravation (e.g. only stopping to get petrol when the light comes on). Romeo would never have stood under Juliet's window reciting poetry if she'd spent all day pashing him behind the stables. He did that stuff because he longed for her company and wasn't allowed to have it whenever it suited him.

Second-rate Shakespearean metaphors aside, my point is that when a man loves you, but feels like he doesn't have you sorted, wrapped up in a bundle and paying half the rent each month, he is more inclined to want to make you his wife.

However, you mustn't think that the fact that he hasn't asked you to move in with him, or hasn't proposed to you, means he doesn't want to give you his last name and make adorable babies with you. In all likeliness, he does. It's simply that you might have made yourself too available.

By living with him, you become his virtual wife. So, ask yourself, what will he get that he isn't already getting if things stay the way they are? And is that enough to make him want to marry you? Chances are, if you're already living with him, the list ain't gonna be very long, or very persuasive.

You have your whole life to wake up next to him and share the BBQ-cleaning duties. You can hold out for another six months.

WHAT HAVE YOU LEARNED?

If you're disillusioned with your current state of affairs, and think that moving in with your fella is the key to moving things along, hopefully you now have some more food for thought to aid your decision. I realise that every couple and every situation is different, but when you're frustrated with inaction you don't always speed things up by . . . speeding things up.

Boost his interest levels by getting back to *you*. Remind yourself that you have a whole lot of other things going on besides your relationship.

By being the girl who refuses to move in until she's engaged, you're indicating that you don't need him to be content, and that he is not responsible for your happiness. He'll see that you cherish a quality relationship, one that doesn't revolve around who is buying the milk, or suspicious hair in the shower drain, but on romance and excitement.

Do you really want to be living with him for another three years before he recognises that he wants to marry you? Or after dropping so many hints, and having become so passive-aggressive about not yet being engaged, that he does it because it's expected of him? Even worse – and I've seen this one several times – you get to a point where your apartment feels too small, and someone wants to start having kids, and even though the finances aren't quite in order, you decide probably getting married is the next logical step. Oh, be still my beating heart! THE ROMANCE IS PARALYSING!

Continue to live apart. Buck the trend. It's a sure-fire way to keep your relationship exciting. Sure, it's annoying to pack a bag each night or rack off at 6 a.m. to go home and get dressed for work, but when those days are gone, and you're drowning in togetherness, you'll look back on them fondly, because life was irregular and unpredictable.

If you already live together and you're dissatisfied with how things have stagnated, move out. Yes, it's going to be a whopping great pain in the arse, and it will feel wrong, painful and like a mini break-up, but it's *not*. Know in your heart that you'll benefit in the end because of your strength and self-respect. You're doing your relationship a favour. You're doing a marvellous, powerful, admirable and bold thing.

You're not being manipulative by wanting to hold out on cohabitation; you're actively prolonging the pleasure of your relationship. Whether you want to get that rock or not, you'll rock.

I have to point out that I don't actually subscribe to the school of thought outlined in this chapter, which is weird, because normally I only have this strong an opinion on food (soggy toast with poached eggs especially).

Holding out to secure a ring isn't quite blackmail, but it's borderline diamondmail. It may well set the foundation for a solid relationship, but it may drastically increase the chances of you visiting a pawn shop with two months of your guy's salary. To some guys, not knowing how you will live together represents not knowing enough facts before making a decision (which any skilled Cluedo player will know is a bad thing).

The key here is: you need to do what it takes to keep the energy in the relationship, it doesn't matter where you're living. I can totally understand how giving a guy everything he wants before marriage, by moving in, might make him less likely to make him bend a knee, but that's why the proposal is special for us. It's because we know how much of a big deal it is. For once, we feel <u>we</u> have all the facts and we aren't doing something because we're scared of missing out, we're doing it because we want in.

Perhaps the lesson of 'don't move in till you get the ring' works best as a metaphor. So you can hold out on cohabitation to force his hand, or move on in and see if he's got what it takes, but either way the message is the same — you've managed to keep it exciting and he wants to lock it down. with a big diamond-shaped lock.

6.

The Relationship Expiry Date

In this lesson, you'll discover that if you are at an age and emotional maturity where you no longer wish to waste time in relationships, there is a finite amount of time you should give a man before you beat it.

Longer than yoghurt (two weeks), shorter than honey (forever).

Do you know a couple who have been together for four, five, six, seven, ten years, and you look at them and you think, 'I *do* love the way they wear the same-coloured tracksuits on Saturdays. It's just adorable'?

They might be part of a sports team who only meet on Saturdays. Look closer.

Then, once you have finished admiring their matching leisure wear, do you stop and think: 'Now, why aren't those two married yet?' Or: 'Why don't they have kids yet?' Or: 'Why don't they buy that little semi they live in?' What on earth could be holding back two people who have been together forever from making some kind of commitment?

I'll tell you what's holding them back. *The fact that they don't want to make some kind of commitment.* He doesn't want to. Or she doesn't want to. Or neither of them do.

It could be because they don't believe in marriage.

Or that he wants to marry her, and she keeps making excuses.

Or that he wants to get married . . . just not to her.

Or that she isn't sure, despite the time they've racked up together, whether he is The One.

Or that he secretly thinks he can do better, or that the grass is greener.

Or that they are so entrenched in their partnership they have forgotten why they are even together.

This is the couple who get assaulted with comments at family functions like: 'When are you two going to make it official?' Or, at weddings or engagements: 'You two are neeee-ext!' Or, at your mum and dad's place: 'When are you going to make an honest woman of my daughter?' And they have to deflect these questions awkwardly because they're: a) too close for comfort; b) encouraging the large elephant in the corner to assert itself; and c) just fucking rude, actually.

If you recognise yourself in this couple, it's time for a reality check.

- How long have you been with this man?
- How in love with him are you, honestly?
- Is it a relationship of familiarity or of fulfilment?
- How likely is it that you think he will propose in the next six months?
- On a scale of 1–10, how do your rate your relationship happiness level?
- Do you look at couples who've been together as long as you and your guy have and yet are married/pregnant/etc., and feel a stab of That Should Be Me?
- Are you disappointed with your boyfriend's

Guys love this. We're always dying for a huge change, in the same way we're always dying for fire ants to be put under our eyelids.

dislike, inability or lack of interest in talking about your future together?

- Do you hear a loud ticking noise and feel a mild flutter of panic?
- Have you been sleeping with his brother?

Even just reading these questions and percolating your answers should give you an indication of where things stand, and whether action is required.

GOOD SIGNS

Reproducing with a loving partner doesn't actually scare all men. We didn't get seven billion humans on earth because guys fear babies.

It's often overlooked, or not given enough considera-tion, that men sometimes accidentally let it slip they think of you as the Mother of Their Children and would be quite thrilled to have you as their wife. (Just *when* is the 790 billion dollar question, but we'll get to that.) The signs may be:

- He has no qualms about attending weddings, and is in fact genuinely happy to do so, and to be part of bridal parties for his mates, or hold and coo at babies.
- He offers his opinions on marriage without being prompted, whether they're regarding religion, church or celebrant, outdoor or indoor, Vegas or City Hall.
- His thoughts are not stuck in the present. He says things like, 'I could live here one day, could you?', or, 'I've always said I'd never put my kids into private schooling because that's where they get fucked up'. This is all kinds of awesome because it indicates he's interested in creating a future with you. (And a less expensive one!)

- He tells you he'll TOTALLY be marrying you one day.

WARNING SIGNS

Sometimes when we're in a relationship, especially one that we have been in for some time, we fail to see the loudest and most neon of signs. This is because after around 18 months a pair of invisible blinkers sneak onto our heads when we're not paying attention. These prevent us from seeing quite alarming things; things that are *fricken obvious in hindsight*, or to close friends with an objective perspective:

- When he hears totally awesome Lady Power songs like 'Single Ladies (Shoulda Put a Ring On It)' he snorts and says, 'God, what a *shit* song'.
- He only discusses friends of his getting engaged with head-shaking, or another-one-bites-the-dustness, or he's-a-bit-young-for-that-isn't-he-wow-I'm-SO-not-in-that-headspace-ness.
- He tells you openly (and perhaps callously), that he doesn't believe in marriage, when he knows you very much do.
- He doesn't think twice before telling you or others that his Grand Plan consists of wanting to travel/move to NYC/London.
- He acts overtly awkward or makes faces when people mention how your kids will look or say things like, 'Surely you two must be about to settle down soon?'.
- His friends are all single and he only hangs out with them because they are so FUN and WILD and AWESOME! Wooh! Tequila time, bitches!

• He says, 'I'm glad I sowed my oats when I was young'. Unless he's a porridge farmer and literally means he's proud of his oat field, this is a GREAT sign, because it will remove a voice in his head urging him to try other girls 23–24 hours a day, even if he's super in love.

- He spells out 'I'M NEVER GOING TO MARRY YOU' with fridge magnets on the freezer.
- You've been living together for more than two years.

That's just a sample. Each man (and woman, let's be fair) has his (or her) own stable of little verbal or non-verbal bombs, some explicit, some tacit. The point is, if you've been in a long-term relationship with a man and he *physically* and/or *verbally* indicates that the idea of committing to you is in some way repellent, or a long way off, or not a priority, and for you it most certainly is, you need to *wake up*.

Within my extended social circle, in the past year I have known of no less than seven long-term relationships breaking down. Of course, each break-up was an entirely independent event, but there was a similar theme trickling through each split: the women wanted more and the men wanted less (or nothing at all).

Guys do tend to view 'something for nothing' as a competitive deal.

I think I can safely say that within this pool of women, most were not prepared to end the relationship *even though their objectives were not being fulfilled, and in all likeliness didn't look they were going to be anytime soon.* And somehow, despite this, the split appeared to come as an enormous shock to them! Then, of course, it tore them apart. And it always does. Because even though they weren't happy, and were living in an 80% relationship, they would have preferred *that* life to one where they have to start all over with a new dude.

Blokes have a habit of pedalling very hard on the Relationship Tandem Bike for the first few months of a relationship, then hope to coast forever. That's why we buzz the back seat, so you hopefully don't see us.

Do not let this be you. Hopefully this book has at least taught you to undertake a certain level of (healthy) analysis and evaluation of your relationship when either your gut or your grey matter indicates something is Not Quite Right.

I have a friend whose boss told her that no performance review should ever come as a surprise: that she should always know *exactly* how she is progressing. Adapt this philosophy to your relationship (despite the fact that there is little chance of a pay rise). Do so *especially* when you are starting to wonder when (or indeed if) he's going to tell you he can't live without you and would like to take steps to ensure you're not left wondering forever.

In short: *talk to him.*

Start by asking him questions of a general nature – in a light, jovial, this-is-not-a-heavy-conversation way – such as, where does he see himself in five years. (Steer VERY clear of questions like 'Where is this relationship headed?', unless you want him to shut down and mentally leave the conversation immediately.) His answer will show you where his head is at, and because there is no explicit talk of marriage/kids, he doesn't feel defensive or uncomfortable and is likely to be more open and honest.

Next, if that went well, you need to ascertain what his *current* thoughts on marriage and kids are. (This can change from year to year, month to month, ratio of single friends to married friends . . .) Maybe mention a friend who just got married or engaged. Remember: keep it super casual. Then, gently segue into when, you know, he might see himself getting married. He might go a bit weird, which could indicate he really hasn't given it much thought before, because he is all happy and situated and if-it-ain't-broke-don't-fixy. If he gives

[handwritten margin note: This is a trick, but like the David Copperfield/ Statue of Liberty one, I rate it.]

you an honest answer, well done! If that answer is 'Oh, goodness, not for a good ten years at least', you know what to do.

ISSUE THE PRIVATE ULTIMATUM

Create an ultimatum in your head. Keep it in there and then *stick to it*.

An example for those girls mad keen to wed might be: 'I'm leaving you in six months if you haven't proposed by then!'

You don't need to tell your boyfriend this date. In fact, if you do, no offence, but you're a moron. Remember that whole 'words speak louder than actions' business? It applies to us, too, especially when it comes to deal breakers. Besides, do you really want to be the girl who cries break-up wolf? *He will not propose because you expect or need him to.* And if you're not willing to walk, don't threaten it. He might have a very good reason for holding off, and your bullying will just propel him the other way.

Think seriously about how long you are prepared to wait, then follow through with your decision if that time limit is not met. All of this waiting, thinking, wasting energy on will-he, and when-will-he, and how-will-he, and oh-it's-my-birthday-it'll-probably-be-tonight, could be far better spent. Don't you think that of the 67 zillion men out there, you can find one who would rather nibble on fermented potatoes than waste time not being married to you?

How much of human life is lost in waiting? – Ralph Waldo Emerson

Probably a good move. We don't want to be pressured, but you don't have forever. It's a classic Mexican standoff, which is no fun for anyone. (I prefer the Mexicans for their waves.)

RELATIONSHIP EXPIRY-O-METER™

1 = STILL FRESH
10 = MORE EXPIRED THAN 12-WEEK-OLD MILK

He says he can't afford a ring/wedding right now = 4
If a man loves you and wants to marry you, he'll give you a plastic ring just to ensure you know he's not going to let any other guy steal in and snaffle you. Sometimes they want to do it properly, and we respect that. However, keep an eye on it . . . After a while, even legitimate reasons like income, not living in a house or 'stuff to sort out', become excuses.

He wants to have all his ducks (usually financial) in a row before getting married = 6
I concede that it's built in to a lot of men's DNA to know they are able to provide for their wife and kids before they accrue a wife and kids. However, this can turn into a never-ending money/security chase, because as soon as most people acquire one goal, they're chasing the next. He can play the money card forever. Some men do.

He says he likes things just the way they are = 10
Some guys (the actual number may be more around 'lots') are both willing and able to stay in a long-term relationship with a woman they love, without any intention of marrying. (I KNOW. Can you believe it? Off with their heads!) This is why we see them splitting from a six-year relationship and then becoming engaged to Another Woman within six months. (Women do this too, of course.) Sadly, you were

Harsh, but it's the same as watching an okay movie – no need to change the channel, but that doesn't make it the one you'd choose for a 'Desert Island'.

unknowingly cast in the play of his life as Being the One Before The One, and it's not a nice feeling.

He claims he is 'not ready' = 9

Men very rarely settle down before they are ready. (This is a blessing – the last thing you want is a guy who has unfinished business bringing his sordid dirt through your house.) And if they do settle down before they're ready, *holy testicle Tuesday* will you find out about it. (Cue resentment, infidelity, disappearing acts, divorce.) What exactly 'ready' means varies, but it tends to revolve around things like having 'sown his wild oats', having enjoyed some freedom/adventure, feeling financially able to provide, having had enough of partying, and looking forward to the next stage of his life. This checklist can take men well into their 70s, especially if they're devastatingly good looking, powerful or wealthy. (S'up, Hef?)

No, it's spelt 'Hame'. I'm such a raconteur.

It's been over five years = 10

How much time do you have, exactly?

DISCLAIMER: Some men are *actually just slow*. Take their time. Spend 25 minutes on the dun' reading the paper. Weigh up 14 quotes before buying a new television. This is the guy who probably plans very much to ask you to saddle up for a ride to Marriage Town, but who just hasn't got around to it yet. If he is a Top Shelf guy, and you love him to pieces, and there's no issue of him being uninterested or unwilling to wed up, because he's totally transparent about his love and future plans with you, you should be willing to sit tight. (For as long as you can handle, anyway.)

Plus, we don't really know what we're doing most of the time, so you have to factor that in.

HOWEVER. If he's making excuses, or being indifferent, or being blatantly uninterested in even the scent of marriage, and you've had a little chat similar to the one recommended earlier, this is probably the moment when you need to take out a pen and some paper, and maybe a glass of Fanta in case you get thirsty, and weigh up exactly how much this relationship is worth to you. How many more months and years are you prepared to wait? It's not about you getting it all your way, and 'your way or the highway', and marry you now or lose you forever – it's about him understanding that just because he gets to *ask* the question, doesn't mean you'll sit around until he decides he feels like doing it.

The dynamic is exactly the same as when the two of you were dating – you're keen and available, but your window of time is finite. You don't need to ask men to marry you, and you don't need to remind them they should.

WHAT HAVE YOU LEARNED?

If marriage (or kids) is important to you, but he's not interested, then you need to seriously consider the possibility that he's not the right man for you. Don't sit there seething at his inaction or becoming increasingly bitter. 'Resentment is like taking poison and waiting for the other person to die,' said Malachy McCourt. (Point: Don't take the poison.)

The alternative is to rethink your own position on marriage. Is it really that important to you? Or are you so hard-wired to *think* it is, that you've forgotten there are other ways to enjoy a long-term, committed relationship with a man? (As far as being an 'official transaction', buying a house together is often harder to extract yourself from than a marriage, for example.) Ultimately, if being with him means more than getting married, then you need to make that decision, deal with it, and never bring up the M word again.

Finally and most importantly, relationships were not intended to be easy, but they were never meant to be hard either. If you're honest with yourself and realise that you do want to get married, or have kids, and you're spending a lot of energy trying to 'assist' your boyfriend to come around to your way of thinking, maybe he's just not the one for you. Maybe you should channel that energy into finding yourself a guy who is equally excited and who needs no convincing whatsoever that you're massively awesome bridal material. There's something to be said for honouring your beliefs. (That something is: 'Go, you.')

FINAL (BRUTAL) THOUGHTS

If the answer to any of these is 'cheese', you should have a snack and come back to it.

Do you think getting married will elevate your relationship somehow?

Do you believe that if he proposes, your life will be perfect?

Is he really the man you want to live with and raise your children with?

Does he love you more than you love him? (Grandma always told me that a man needs to love you 2% more than you do him.)

Does he make you feel beautiful?

Are you yourself around him? Or do you censor certain parts of who you are?

Are you happy within yourself, or are you waiting for marriage to 'make you happy'?

What's in this marriage for you?

Instead of focusing on why doesn't he want to marry you, ask why you want to marry *him*.

Are you changing your behaviour to appear 'marriageable'?

Are you so busy playing Perfect Girlfriend you have forgotten how to be an Awesome Woman?

Do you think he'll want to marry you more if you talk about it a lot?

As long as you talk about things with your guy, he'll never resent you for doing what you have to do to be happy. A lot of girls have extensive board meetings in their heads for hours on end, and the only bit we guys hear is the press release. Let us into your head (not literally – we might wear muddy shoes) and you can expect a much more balanced joint goal.

7.

Happily Never Afters

In this lesson, you'll learn how to elegantly move on from a relationship that you now see was not serving your journey.

At this point you may have been proposed to and are planning your Day of Days. *Congratulations!* I'm thrilled to my frills for you. Thank you for your time and all the very, very best to you both for your life together. (PS Whatever you do, do NOT seat the single people with the widowed grandparents at the wedding. This is cruel and unusual punishment for not having a partner.)

Or else, despite wanting it very much, no offer of a formal commitment has been forthcoming. If so, it's a case of: ball, court, yours.

If things are cruising along in your relationship peacefully and blissfully, then bravo. Enjoy yourselves, you loved-up little so-and-sos.

If you're filled with discontent, frustration and what-ifs, or find yourself groaning 'too long' when people ask how long the two of you have been together, then something needs to be done.

This is the business end of the book. We have educated you about how to love and value yourself, how to attract quality men and how to enjoy a balanced, interesting relationship where both parties feel they bring something to the table, and it is wholly appreciated by their partner. We have taught you how to maintain your glow even in the thick of an all-consuming relationship and we have (hopefully) advised you on how to create an environment where your boyfriend feels compelled to commit to you, because obviously you're a Total Catch.

All of this stuff is about growth.

But unfortunately, the most valuable personal development is usually accompanied by some form of discomfort, pain or difficulty. Like ending a relationship, for example. Or having it ended for you. ←

Our gut always indicates when a relationship is not healthy, but we become very good at ignoring it. But why would you choose (and it's always a choice) to remain in a relationship that makes you unhappy? Are you scared of being alone? Lonely? Viewed as a failure?

Of course, it's not always as easy as packing up your backpack and scarpering off into the sunset.* In fact, it's kind of never easy. Dumpee or dumper. Sometimes there are even houses and children involved, which further sways you to perhaps stay and try to make it work. Sometimes you genuinely love each other but you can both see it's not working. Sometimes you think it's all going well and then from left field comes a Dear John letter and an emotional kick up the arse.

So. Consider your current relationship. Honestly. Brutally.

For just $39.95 you can text a code and zoë will do it on your behalf within 24 hours, and you get a free thermos. (Not really — that would be a cop-out on your behalf. And our thermos contact fell through.)

*For one, the sunset is actually thousands of kilometres away.

Do you, or does he, for whatever reason, feel it's not working? That inactivity is no longer an option? It might be that things are stagnant. Or you wish for more and he doesn't. Or he wishes for more and you don't. Perhaps you feel he is trespassing against your relationship in some way, or that if you stay with him you'll be bound to a situation that offers you only 70% of the happiness you know you could be feeling? Have you been working so hard on the relationship or yourself that you are exhausted? *What does your gut tell you about this?*

Does it want cheese? Again, take a snack break.

Can you look yourself in the mirror and say: *This partnership serves my growth and happiness and I know there is no better relationship for me at this time?*

If you feel the answer is yes, then cleanse those demons and off we go! Maybe start by listing all the things you love about Your Guy and getting yourself back into a positive frame of mind. When you start acting with an overriding sense of gratitude and love, your perspective shifts real fast. It also influences how Your Guy will behave – there's nothing more attractive than feeling your partner beaming appreciation and love at you.

Important: If you've made a conscious decision to Give This Thing a Go, then that's exactly what you need to do. No more bringing up past incidents. No more digs about that time that chick sat on his lap, or when he forgot to pick you up that night. This has to be a CLEAN SLATE. No grudge-bearing allowed. *A relationship riddled with resentment or bitterness cannot succeed.*

Sometimes when girls think they're giving a clean slate, there're still a few crumbs left on it. Not to be picky, but we notice it very quickly. (Unlike real crumbs in the kitchen, which we cannot see.)

If you feel the answer is no, it could be time to initiate a 'change of circumstances'. Look at this change not as something scary and awful, but as an opportunity for growth. You grow the most from facing the things you fear the most. Comfort and familiarity should not be the reason you are staying in a relationship. And just because you have a past with this man, it does not imply you have a future with him. What have you really got to lose, and what do you stand to gain?

And the day came when the risk to remain tight in a bud was more painful than the risk it took to blossom – Anaïs Nin.

Good one, Ninster.

DATING DICTIONARY: INTUITION MODE

Intuition Mode is the mental state achieved when a woman remembers how powerful and helpful her 'sixth sense' – AKA her gut feeling – actually is, and then starts paying attention to it, instead of trying to intellectualise things as she usually does.

Usually our intuition tells us what we should do long before we actually do it. (Like when you just know taking that job with that nice man with the gold tooth, white dress shoes and three mobile phones is probably not the wisest career move.) Your intuition is a tool all women should harness. Just like a good-quality hair dryer and a phenomenal black lacy bra. Here's an example:

ACTION: Carmella starts going through Donald's phone/email/pockets when he's not around because she has a hunch he is cheating on her, or gambling, or doing the drugs he promised he wouldn't do anymore, or illegally importing toucans again.

EXPLANATION: Snooping generally provides fuel for fires that you *really* don't want burning because, unfortunately, if you think you'll find something, you usually will. So for Carmella to have made the conscious decision to go through Donald's things looking for some kind of proof that he was doing the wrong thing by her, on some level, indicates she feels it probably *is* happening, and now all that's needed is the evidence. (The shitty part of snooping is that should you find some evidence, his fury over your 'detective work' will often override the validity of your proof. Meaning that neither of you now trust the other. Brilliant!) Suffice to say, snooping is less like opening a can of worms, and more like opening a can of serpents with laser-beams shooting from their eyes and ultrasonic hissing that makes your ears bleed. Proceed with caution.

years of watching cop shows have taught us the term 'inadmissible evidence', which we enjoy using because it makes us feel like Jimmy Smits, or anyone else from 'NYPD Blue'.

ASSESSMENT: Carmella needs to stop trying to crack that Gmail account and ask herself *why she is doing this*. What's the bigger issue? There must be distrust and/or insecurity present for her to be probing around in his stuff. What has triggered her intuition? Is it something she has spoken to Donald about already but she felt he was deceiving her? Did a friend tell her something? Or is she just 'going with her gut' to see what she finds?

EXCEPTIONS: If he never lets his phone out of sight (takes it into the bathroom with him, locks it permanently), gets funny whenever you walk up behind him when he is on his computer, won't let you *use* his computer, is shady about where he went out or with whom, or you catch him out in lies, then the activation of Intuition Mode is entirely appropriate. Usually, if something looks or feels a bit suss, it is. (A tattoo of another girl's name suddenly appearing on his bicep, for instance.)

Unless her name is 'Mum'.

RESOLUTION: Once Carmella understands *why* she is snooping, she needs to instigate an honest conversation with Donald about her fears. They might be completely unfounded, or based on miscommunication, and he deserves a chance to defend himself. If he reacts in an overly defensive fashion, or in a way that makes Carmella's Intuition Mode blare with piercing warning sirens, she needs to weigh up whether she is prepared to take action, or stay in a relationship that doesn't sit right with her.

This battle of brain versus instinct can take years to climax. Some women demand physical proof before leaving a relationship, even though there is a relentless whisper in the back of their mind saying, 'All is not well'. Some see the proof and stay anyway. Some ditch as soon as they realise this situation won't heal until they get the proof, and that it may never come, and they simply can't wait that long. It's entirely personal. However, always remember that we women were bestowed with the gift of intuition for a reason. Yes, it was mostly to aid us in protecting our children from being killed by sabre-tooth tigers, but it also exists to protect *us*. It's the thing that kicks in when you're faced with a dark alley. With a menacing taxi driver.

Very similar to how Peter Parker didn't like Spider Senses at first, but then embraced them and the rest was history. (Pretend history.)

With a dodgy-looking hotel in Turkey. It is a powerful tool and should not be underestimated. Many a woman has ended a relationship and then wondered why they fought their intuition for so long. But we always act when it's right for us. Don't be hard on yourself. Be hard on your relationship.

Relevant song lyric: 'If what they say is "Nothing is forever", then what makes, then what makes, then what makes, then what makes, then what makes love the exception?' ('Hey Ya', OutKast)

CHECKLIST

Are you prolonging the inevitable? Or is this relationship worth saving and you're just going through a shitty patch? Check off those that apply to you.

- You don't wake up with a smile and a pep in your step anymore.
- You're tired. Fed up. Long for easier times.
- You make excuses for his behaviour constantly.
- People don't really want to hang out with you two, because you generally end up bickering or bitching each other out.
- Your friends no longer offer you relationship advice, because you don't take it.
- You're engaging in self-destructive behaviour or avoidance techniques.
- You look at other couples and can't help wondering why *your* relationship isn't that good (even though you know you shouldn't play comparisons, because every couple has their own seedy undercurrent going on).

- You don't discuss your future together.
- You feel obliged to make contact, rather than feeling enthused. Or he does.
- You secretly fantasise about being single again, and you're envious of your single friends' stories.
- It hurts. Relationships that hurt don't need to be saved, they need to be exterminated.
- You've started up an email relationship with a workmate when you know it's inappropriate.
- You're going out more, whether it's because you're yearning for independence, craving attention or just for some fun and excitement.
- You're feeling bored, pent-up, distracted and you're snapping at your boyfriend without provocation.
- There is lying or secrets.
- Your boyfriend has changed. Can't put your finger on what. Goes out more. Surly and distant.
- You two fight. A lot.
- You two aren't having sex. At all.
- Things you used to adore about him now irritate you.
- You start to realise that 'hard' isn't code for 'passionate', it just means 'hard'.
- Your fights are dirty. Personal attacks run rife.
- You don't make an effort for each other anymore.
- You forecast a year ahead and can't see how anything will change.
- You accidentally got married to a man wearing a novelty moustache on a girls' trip to Vegas.

Of course, there are 2489 other reasons that aren't listed here but might pertain to your relationship and your feelings regarding your relationship, but I think you get the gist and will start to see what's really going on.

LESS COMMON REASONS PEOPLE BREAK UP

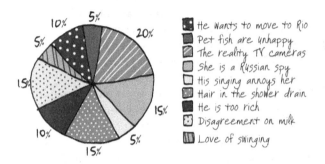

He wants to move to Rio
Pet fish are unhappy
The reality TV cameras
She is a Russian spy
His singing annoys her
Hair in the shower drain
He is too rich
Disagreement on milk
Love of swinging

DECISION TIME: STAY OR GO?

I can't counsel on this. Sorry. This part is up to you. I'm just going to sit here and watch *Entourage* re-runs till you've figured out what you're going to do. No rush! Take your time. I've got enough pita bread and hummus here to last me until hovercars are the preferred mode of transport.

WHEN TWO BECOME ONE

If you're reading this paragraph, I'll assume your decision was of the break-up variety. (Ouch.) Or of the you-were-broken-up-with variety. (Extended remix ouch.) Either way, here are some handy hints to help you find your way through what is never much fun to begin with. In fact, it's AWFUL, HEART-WRENCHING, SOUL-DESTROYING stuff. And you fear you may actually die. Or kill somebody. You oscillate between desperate, aching hollowness and all-consuming rage. Food loses all taste. Alcohol seems to gain more taste. Life is clouded in a veil of gloom. *You can all go to hell.*

But then something shifts. Suddenly you're laughing at Peter the IT Guy's shit jokes again. You start saying yes to invites. Life becomes fun and exciting, and you get to go back to the start of this book and read all that empowering stuff about being Positively Selfish and flirty again!

But first, let's get you through that first bit. (Maybe put the bottle of shiraz down just for a moment so you can focus on the words.)

[handwritten margin note: Be warned though, Peter the IT Guy will think he's definitely in with a chance during this period.]

THE BREAK-UP RULE: DON'T BE CRAZY, BE COOL

Whether you're on the passive end of a break-up (i.e. he broke up with you), or it was mutual, or even if you pulled the plug, things can swiftly escalate from 'dealing with it' to 'destroying his personal effects'.

Even if you understand the reasons for the break-up, even if you agree with them, even if you know it's For The Best – it doesn't matter. *We're all capable of majorly losing our shit.*

Examples of Majorly Losing Our Shit
- Keying 'fucker' onto the bonnet of his car.
- Hacking into his Facebook and changing his status to read: 'Sad that he is the worst lay in the world.'

- Calling his friends to scream and demand the truth, or just to scream in general.
- Tweeting, Lindsay Lohan–style, about what a tool he is, incessantly, for weeks.
- Sleeping with his flatmate – while he's in the lounge room.
- Turning up at his work in a mess, begging for him to take you back.
- Sending him violent, angry, screamy emails and texts.
- Sprinkling grass seed on his carpet and then watering it, creating an Apartment Park.
- Turning up to his place, drunk, at 3 a.m., demanding a conversation, or sex or Scotch (or a sexy Scotch? Sean Connery perhaps?).

All of these things, by the way, confirm our decision. Like throwing away an apple because it had a worm in it, then a rabid rat crawls out, too.

Some people mistakenly think Post-Break-up Behaviour is not included in the list of things that define your character, or reflect who you truly are as a person. Regrettably, it is *precisely* how we react in unhappy or hard times that truly define who we are. Which means that just because you're stinging with hurt and jittery with rage, you're not allowed to indulge in behaviour that suggests evidence of heavy pharmaceutical abuse or mental instability. Being hurt doesn't make you exempt from reprimand, accountability or judgement. (Or in some cases, prosecution. Because surprisingly, setting fire to his house is still against the law, even if he did cheat on you then dump you for her. I know! Ridiculous.)

So maybe, just before you cut up that Dior Homme suit or hit send on that email to everyone on your contacts list (with a picture of him and a diatribe about how he has herpes, and everyone should warn their girlfriends to away from him), stop and forecast how awesome and clever this action will look in 12 months time. Will you be proud or ashamed? Are you being a mature, intelligent human being? How will this affect you karmically? And *what if Santa Claus finds out?*

What feels *so right* when you are in a highly emotional state is rarely right at all. **Do not act.** Think it, visualise it, even write it down, but *do not act.* Your inaction will be rewarded with eternal peace of mind, and your police record will stay pristine. Win–win.

When I was going through a particularly gnarly break-up (angry as hell, frothing and chomping at the bit to unleash a tirade of explosives), mum wisely told me that getting angry is like spitting in the wind – it always comes back to you. Thank God she told me this, because once you send that email, or make the phone call, or finish that graffiti on his car, *you can't get it back.*

Spit some venom. By all means, get it out. But spit it all out privately, or with your girlfriends, then hold that head up high again. You will be so very glad you did. No one wants to be That Crazy Ex-Girlfriend.

BREAK UP WITH ELEGANCE

The chief break-up goal should always be to walk away with grace. Even if you're dying inside, there is such beauty, strength and splendour in walking out of an agonising break-up with your chin tilted towards the sky. Of course you're hurting. Feel sick with upset. Confused. Shocked. *This is all okay.* Grieve. Throw shit. Yell. (Not at him, remember.) Take it one day

It might put a hole in your karma barrel, which is bad. The good news is, there is no such thing as a karma barrel.

Remember what Confucius said: 'whoever flips out first in a break-up will look like a real goose next week.' It wasn't one of his more famous sayings, but I think he nailed it.

at a time and try not to punch people who tell you they always thought he was a schmuck, and there are plenty more fucking fish in the sea.

There is this great anonymous saying: 'I'm going to smile and make you think I'm happy, I'm going to laugh, so you don't see me cry. I'm going to let you go in style, and even if it kills me – I'm going to smile.'

And good *Lord* this is a terrific mantra to adopt when you're untangling yourself from a relationship. Write it out and pin it to your mirror! Memorise it! Live by it!

Or write it backwards and stick it on the wall opposite your mirror!

Here's why:

1. You're being cool, not crazy.
2. It gives your ex zero ammunition to believe he did the right thing by breaking it off. Acting crazy gives him *plenty*.
3. There is an irresistible allure associated with detachment. It serves you because you get the all-important space you need after a break-up. And while I'm not here to tell you how to get him back (both literally and figuratively), playing it cool, *almost to the point of being clinical,* is the most powerful tool in your artillery.
4. The concept of 'fake it till you make it' may feel contrived, or like you're lying to yourself, but plastering a smile on your face and affirming mentally that you're doing well has a powerful effect on your state of mind.
5. The less drama you inject into a break-up, the quicker you can move on. Telling people you're a mess and can't eat, and that he has ruined you, will perpetuate these emotions.

Remember: you're doing a very brave thing. You're amazing. Don't forget that it is letting go that makes you strong, not holding on.*

*The opposite of Rock Climbing Rule #1.

COMMON BREAK-UP MISTAKES

You want him back and you make this very clear to him

Are you sure? What will have changed if you get back together? Will you be able to forgive and forget? Honestly? Okay. None of my business. Generally if you go backwards you fall over, but hey, this is your life. If you want him back, or you believe there is hope for reconciliation, the only way to proceed is to act as if you don't. Make him think it's over for good. Make him question why you're not asking him to give things another chance. Don't allow him to sit there, cocky, knowing you're fixated with getting him back. Golly, is *that* a recipe for disaster! It goes back to all that stuff we discussed about men (and women) being infinitely more attracted to that which is hard to obtain, over that which is served up on a platter with a Post-it note saying 'I live for you'. Remember: Men don't respond to words, they respond to no contact. Also remember (if you're game): A break-up is like broken glass. It is better to leave it broken than hurt yourself fixing it.

Unless you broke up with him, but you can only do this once. Otherwise we'll think you're just going to keep doing it. Like when people do the 'walkout' when they're buying a car.

You think you can stay friends

Here's why that's a stinker: you can't. You just can't. Not now. And you know this because you've seen enough TV shows where this ends up in tears to know better. But you're so devastated at losing this person from your life in such a violent manner that even a terrible, painful faux friendship would be better than moving on. (If he still wants you, the 'friendship' disguise is a commonly used one. Like being kicked out of a club and then coming back in a different hat – it doesn't change the person.) The problem is that one party always has more attachment than the other, or an agenda – it is very, very, very rarely an even playing field. People can become very selfish when they know someone is desperate to have them – in any form – in their lives. Cue convenience sex, Sunday night pretend boyfriend–girlfriend couch time, late-night calls or texts that utterly confuse the weaker party . . . It's unhealthy and never comes to any good. Cut the cord. Move forward. When you're both in a clean headspace, or in a relationship with another person, then – and only then – can you *maybe* rekindle a basic friendship. The ideal situation is being at peace with your relationship – and break-up – and having a mutual respect for each other. (If he was an arsehole, maybe just aim for the 'at peace' bit.)

If you break up with a guy and he still wants to be 'friends', roughly 20000% of the time it's because he's hoping you'll fall back in love with him. Sometimes the percentage is a bit less, but not by much.

- Showing up to the same party and having a nervous breakdown/a fight with him/leaving immediately – work to be done.
- Showing up to the same party, saying hi, maybe having a brief, polite chat and then each carrying on and having a good night – healthy.
- Showing up to the same party, not wanting to leave his side, ashing your cigarette in his date's drink – unhealthy.

You dart directly into another guy's arms

You've administered a cheap band-aid and you're not dealing with your break-up. You're procrastinating.

You're allowing your vulnerable, needy side to triumph, and failing to see the long-term benefits of self-control and time to get over the last guy. You're jamming all of your sadness and hurt in a cupboard and refusing to deal with it, preferring instead the excitement and rush of a new lover. Of course, this cupboard will force open eventually. You've allowed yourself no time to process or heal. You're happy initially, but this will not last. Also, it's unfair to the New Guy (AKA the 'transitory dater'). In short: a shitty idea.

WHAT HAVE YOU LEARNED?

You would not have broken up unless there were problems. Big ones. But it is not the end of the world. It really isn't. Recognise your part in the break-up, be honest about what went wrong and why, and then learn from this so you don't repeat the same mistakes.

I believe that break-ups are gifts in disguise. (What? You didn't see the cloak and novelty moustache?) You can use them as an excuse to stay miserable if you like, but even your darkest hour is only 60 minutes long.

Although I may be taken out the back of the shelter sheds and given a severe Chinese burn by the International Man Organisation for revealing this, the simple truth is — if you want a guy to have a mental breakdown after a break-up, act as happy as Larry. Every smile you flash at the world will kick his ego right in the groin. (Yes, even our egos have groins.)

8.

Ignore Everything In This Book

In this lesson, you'll be reminded of the fact that we can only offer you our advice – it's up to you what you do with it.

Now that you're all informationatised you must be gagging to try all of your awesome new life lessons. Just remember: these lessons don't and won't apply to everyone.* Every person, situation and relationship is unique and you should always do what you feel and believe is best and right for you.

*No refunds though, obviously.

Unless it's stupid, in which case you should do what we recommend instead. Here's what that was again, just in case you fell asleep and missed some.

SELF-CONFIDENCE IS PARAMOUNT

The lessons in this book are *impossible* to follow unless you have built a core of solid self-confidence and self-love. Seriously. Do you think you will be able to let calls and texts go unanswered from a new suitor unless you have high self-esteem, a solid understanding of who you are and of your greatest assets, and the knowledge that you are worth chasing? (If you answered yes, please return to page 1 and start again. If you answered no, and kind of loudly, in a hallelujah fashion, special bonus points to you.)

KNOW YOUR WORTH

Are you feeling and looking as good as you can? Do you hold yourself with confidence? Do you have a good outlook on your life? Are you pro-men? Are you open to new experiences? Can you weigh up what you bring to a relationship and feel like you are an atomic catch (and be honest: if you know you still have trust or jealousy issues from your last relationship, maybe work on that a little more before jumping into a new relationship)?

Are you living the kind of active, full life that means you aren't looking for a man to bring you excitement and happiness? Can you walk into a party and feel confident, happy and irresistible? Can you do the worm at this party? Without mussing up your hair? Holy shit, you're amazing. *I'd* date you.

BE CLEAR ABOUT WHAT YOU WANT

And not just when it comes to new-season handbags or sandwich options. You know precisely what kind of man and relationship you want, which means that you have a much, much better chance of actually attracting it.

ENJOY BEING CHASED

Firstly because you know you're worth being chased, and second because you know that men always respond more favourably to a challenge than when something is too readily available. Making the first move never pays off for women, and a little anticipation never killed *anyone*. Most importantly, though, if you enthuse him to chase you, in the end, you both win – he 'conquers' you, and you feel like a prize that has been won.

IF HE CALLS, THEN HE EXISTS

If he doesn't, well, he doesn't. Simple. After all, I'm pretty sure you've got better shit to do with your time than check your phone 569 times a day, and miss out on fun with your friends and family just because Some Guy you met might call.

CONTROL THE PACE

If Modern Guy had it his way, you would be together four of the first seven nights after having met. This sounds romantic, but as Elvis's body mass kindly demonstrated just before his death, too much of a good thing is usually too much of a good thing. Hold the reins, pump the brakes and enjoy the courting period. Familiarity breeds contempt. Absence makes the heart grow fonder. You'll usually have to be the one to instigate this, as men sometimes fail to realise that when they get to see you every day for two weeks, seeing you won't seem so special anymore.

Stick to your guns and space out your dates, even when it's killing you because you want to see him 25 hours a day. It will boost your appeal and benefit your (potential) relationship.

SET LIMITS AND STICK TO THEM

Expectations – particularly those regarding SMS, email or telephone contact – are an enormous cause of anguish for a lot of women. So LET GO OF THEM. Set strong boundaries for how long you're willing to indulge Mr No Contact and then get on with your life if you feel like he's having a lend, or is just not worth the energy. *Women have actually died of hunger waiting for texts to come through about dinner dates.* People respect those who respect them-selves – and never is this more pertinent than when you've had four wines and he hasn't texted in three days and you fire off a textoid that you really, really shouldn't have.

PAY MIND TO ACTIONS, NOT WORDS

Ever made breakfast plans for the next morning with someone after a few drinks? Ever actually followed through on those plans? (You did? *Liar.*) Talking is incredibly easy to do; following through takes a little more effort. The inconsistency between the two is one of the best ways to ascertain a person's character, so pay attention to what Your Boyfriend does, instead of what he says, and you'll soon see what kind of person you are really dealing with.

KEEP YOUR ROMANCE ROMANTIC

Showing him your tracksuit pants within two weeks of meeting him seems cute and adorable and cosy, but you can never get back the Pre-Tracksuit Era once you leave it. Draw out the romance and the excitement of dating for as long as you can. Show each other your Romance Artillery and set the standard for the future. You've got years to sprawl over the lounge on a Saturday night watching DVDs.

STOP MAKING EXCUSES

He never comes to *your* family stuff. Never calls you to let you know he's running late. Keeps telling you he'll quit smoking. Lets you down and appears to not really care that you're upset. These might all seem insignificant alone, but they add up over time. Be aware of how often you make excuses for him and be brutal about how much effort he is really injecting into this relationship. Remember: it takes 23 seconds to send a text message. And if he can't manage that, well maybe you need to assess exactly how awesome he really is. You teach people how they treat you, so teach him well.

MAKE IT OFFICIAL

After dating for a while and realising you're quite smitten with each other, usually there is a need for a 'chat' so that you can check you're both on the same page. The Relationship Defining Chat (RDC) is important because it signals you are now Exclusive with each other and can no longer trot off and sleep with your ex-boyfriend anymore (you) or order multiple lap dances on a night out (him). It's that moment when you both say, 'Yes! I would like to give this a go!' (except really quietly, awkwardly and quickly, and with lots of tension-diffusing humour), and it's crucial, because you both deserve to know where you stand.

MAINTAIN YOUR PRE-GUY LIFE

The temptation to completely merge your life with his is typhoon-strong when you're frolicking about in those heady New Relationship days, but resistance is key. Keep up your social activities. Maintain your friendships. Don't stop your daily walk or drift away from the gym. It's these things that made you so happy – and hence so attractive – when he met you, and giving them up to immerse yourself in the Boyfriend Cave is the antithesis of a mutually satisfying, well-rounded relationship. Men (and women) prefer a partner who doesn't rely on them for all their entertainment and happiness needs. Self-sufficiency is underrated.

YOU CANNOT CHANGE A MAN

Men come to you one way and that very rarely changes. We women often feel it is a display of love for us to want to 'help' our boyfriends to be better, or dress better, or strive for that promotion, but men usually just interpret that to mean we think they're inadequate. So, treat him as you would a friend: don't nag. Don't belittle him. Let him be and love him for who he is. Appreciate all the good he does. Lovingly (genuinely) massage his ego, demonstrate your gratitude and watch the change in his attitude. (If he still leaves his wet towel on the bed after all that, you have every right to go apeshit.)

KEEP IT ROMANTIC, NOT DOMESTIC

Being in each other's faces all the time is *not the key to a great relationship*. It's the key to familiarity, and often resentment or boredom. So avoid it! Commit to a relationship based on quality not quantity! Complement, don't complete each other! This is especially pertinent for those wanting to move things onto The Next Level: a large part of attraction is mystery, and when you live together, that mystery disappears. Do not mistakenly think that by being around him more, showing him 'how it could be', he'll fall over himself to propose. It's hard for a man to 'lock you down' and make you his woman forever if you're already sitting in the chair with the padlock in place and the key in your mouth.

KNOW WHEN IT'S OVER

A lot of this book has pushed the idea of creating and sticking to boundaries. Of knowing when your situation is serving your journey, and when it is prohibiting it. This means you should be well equipped to call it off if you can see your relationship is not heading where you want it to. Be honest with each other about his and your needs, set a private ultimatum, and then act accordingly.

MOVE ON WITH GRACE

It is never easy to instigate a break-up, or to be showered with the unique brand of hurt, dismissal and ache of having someone break up with you. However. Break-ups always occur for a reason. And, surprisingly, that reason is not for you to demonstrate just how psychotic you can really be. Even if you're saturated with rage, keep your cool. Elegance cannot be underestimated when the sweet cream of your love turns sour. Neither can changing his name in your phone to 'DO NOT CALL OR ANSWER THIS NUMBER'.

FINAL HILARIOUS GRAPH TO LIGHTEN THE MOOD

Most Common Feedback on this Book

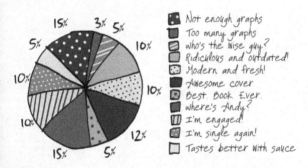

I have nothing of any value to say here, but you'd be well aware that hasn't seemed to stop me yet, so why would it now? Thanks for reading, sorry for the interruptions. I thought zoë's bits were great.

Further Reading

Self-confidence a little shaky? Heart a little bit breaky? Here's some before- and after-reading for these periods. And a virtual high-five for braving the look you'll get at the counter when you buy them.

Preparation
The Power of Now, Eckhart Tolle
A New Earth, Eckhart Tolle
Secrets About Life Every Woman Should Know, Barbara De Angelis
The Power of Your Subconscious Mind, Dr Joseph Murphy
The Secret (on CD and DVD too), Rhonda Byrne
The Meta-Human: A Handbook for Personal Transformation, Paul Solomon
Sex and Psychic Energy (this is not a joke suggestion), Betty Bethards

Happily Never Afters
How to Heal a Broken Heart in 30 Days: A Day-by-Day Guide to Saying Good-bye and Getting On With Your Life, Howard Bronson and Mike Riley
Extreme Breakup Recovery, Jeanette Castelli
It's Called a Breakup Because It's Broken: The Smart Girl's Break-Up Buddy, Greg Behrendt and Amiira Ruotola-Behrendt
It's A Breakup Not A Breakdown: Get over the big one and change your life – for good!, Lisa Steadman

Acknowledgements

Thank you to the Emperor Penguins, Kirsten, Rachel and Michael, for being so wonderfully enthusiastic and supportive of this book, and for (foolishly) giving me such a dazzling virtual soapbox from which to preach outrageous relationship instruction. Thank you to all my dear, exceptional friends for allowing me to rant and rave about these philosophies, and for only laughing at my zeal some of the time. A special thanks must also go to those friends whose emotional torture provided me with the ideal vessel to test my advice (and to make you feel really bad about yourself for texting him when you shouldn't have). I recognise how twisted this sounds, but sitting with you in your ouchiest, most frustrating relationship moments and being able to inject you with some strength and perspective, gave me the confidence to realise that maybe I was okay at this advice thing. Thank you mum, for passing on your unhealthy obsession with self-help books, and, oh yeah – for offering me incredibly powerful and pure relationship counsel my entire life. I wouldn't have dared write such a book without your wisdom and insight safely tucked into my back pocket. (It's not plagiarism if it's family, right?) Finally, thank you, Hamebot for your emotionally evolved male back-up vocals, for being the world's funniest (and funnest) co-pilot and for lifting the hilarity/enjoyment/entertainment levels of this book to stratospheric levels. We done good.

read more

my penguin e-newsletter

Subscribe to receive *read more*, your monthly e-newsletter from Penguin Australia. As a *read more* subscriber you'll receive sneak peeks of new books, be kept up to date with what's hot, have the opportunity to meet your favourite authors, download reading guides for your book club, receive special offers, be in the running to win exclusive subscriber-only prizes, plus much more.

Visit penguin.com.au/readmore to subscribe